Essential
Costa del Sol

by

GEORGE KEAN

George Kean is an experienced travel writer
who lives and works in Spain. He is the author
of three Spanish titles in the current series of
Essential guides.

G000270572

AA

Produced by AA Publishing

Written by George Kean
Peace and Quiet section
by Paul Sterry
Series Adviser: Ingrid Morgan
Series Controller: Nia Williams
Copy Editor: Antonia Hebbert

Edited, designed and produced by
AA Publishing. Maps ©
The Automobile Association 1992

Distributed in the United Kingdom
by the Publishing Division of The
Automobile Association, Fanum
House, Basingstoke, Hampshire,
RG21 2EA

The contents of this publication are
believed correct at the time of
printing. Nevertheless, the
publishers cannot accept
responsibility for errors or
omissions, nor for changes in details
given. We have tried to ensure
accuracy in this guide, but things do
change and we would be grateful if
readers could advise us of any
inaccuracies they may encounter.

A CIP catalogue record for this book
is available from the British Library.

ISBN 0 7495 0304 1

Published by The Automobile
Association

Typesetting: Microset Graphics Ltd,
Basingstoke
Colour separation: BTB Colour
Reproduction, Whitchurch,
Hampshire
Printed in Italy by Printers SRL,
Trento

Front cover picture: Nerja

This book employs a simple rating system to help choose which places to visit:

◆◆◆ do not miss

◆◆ see if you can

◆ worth seeing if you have time

INTRODUCTION

For providing pleasure and release in the sun for many millions of pale Europeans, Spain's 'Coast of the Sun' deserves the highest praise. For ugly over-development in some parts, business people and public authorities of the past must be criticised; but today's administrators have recognised previous errors and are trying to make amends. From the 1970s, the European package holiday industry fired a demand for rampant development. Central government was hungry for foreign investment and exchange, so development went on though the authorities had not the plans nor the money to provide an adequate infrastructure, nor enough officials with foresight and concern for the environment. Now the travel industry has changed. There is growing recognition that speculators must be controlled and the infrastructure improved, and that ecology must become a major concern. Thankfully, all these things are happening along the Costa del Sol.

Enlightenment architects created the Puente Nuevo spanning the Tajo Gorge at Ronda

The name applies to 100 miles (160km) of coastline in Málaga province within the region of Andalucía, one of Spain's 17 Autonomous Communities. Together with Andalucía's other seven provinces, Málaga is changing as it moves into the 21st century. It is as if the whole region is making a fast, united march of socio-economic progress, within the largest regional development programme ever envisaged in the European Community. A new brood of officials is about: better-trained people with deeper insight and greater foresight. Some will say that this view is too optimistic, particularly the popular media of Britain and other European countries. Regularly writers and reporters arrive on 'freebies' and return with horror stories and tales of woe. Like other coastal strips and islands of Spain, Europe's most popular country for vacations, the Costa del Sol is very prominent in the consciousness of readers and viewers, and media people

Benalmádena Costa is typical of many resort developments along the coast

Málaga has grown along the narrow coastal land strip between the sierras and the shores of the Mediterranean

know that bad news attracts more attention. The Costa del Sol deserves better than that, however. Yes, it does have blemishes and problems, and this book will not attempt to hide them. But it remains a place that offers something for everyone, whatever their age or economic status – not only the seaside resorts but also the fascinating hinterland and beguiling cities which can easily be discovered on day trips from the resorts. It is also a place to visit outside the peak summer season. With Europe's most evenly balanced climate, the Costa del Sol is an all-year destination.

At its centre is the provincial capital city of Málaga, which is well worth getting to know. Most of the coastline to the west is not particularly attractive and the beaches cannot be rated highly. But the almost continuous 'lateral city' along this coast is packed with swimming pools, golf courses and other high-standard sports facilities, good shopping, eating places and nightspots, in urbanisations and resorts of every standard and price choice. East of Málaga lies La Axarquía district, an enchanting mix of old and new, with a lot of natural beauty.

BACKGROUND

Over 25,000 years ago, Stone Age man walked the shores and inhabited caves along the Costa del Sol. Around 1000BC, Phoenicians were trading with the local Iberians. Greeks arrived 400 years later to set up commercial colonies. Soon they were displaced by Carthaginians from North Africa. When they began their conflict with Rome in the First Punic War (264–241BC), the Carthaginians were also under attack by the Iberians. In the Second Punic War (219–201BC) southern Iberia was a major area of fighting. The Romans won and for 600 years imposed their sovereignty over what they named Baetica. They began building aqueducts, roads and cities (remnants of which remain), and their language, legal and civil codes became the base for those now existing in Spain. Christianity filtered in during the 1st century, and in AD306 all Roman citizens gained religious freedom. Rome's empire disintegrated slowly and early in the 5th century Baetica was overrun by the Germanic tribe called the Vandals. They were soon chased to North Africa by allies of Rome, the Visigoths, who were also Germanic but were converts to Arianism, the Christianity of Byzantium. In AD475 Rome conceded that the Visigoths were rulers of what had been its Iberian provinces. The Visigoths took up Roman ways, and in 590 Roman Catholicism became their state religion. Their numbers were few however, and constant rivalry among their military aristocracy and elected monarchy undermined their rule. In 711, the Visigoths were defeated in battle on the banks of the Río Guadalete (Cádiz province) by the army of Moors led by Tarik. The Moors were Muslims from North Africa. They ruled for the next 780 years over what they named Al-Andalus, bringing advanced administration, knowledge about agriculture and fine architecture. It is the legacy of the long Moorish presence in the region which today distinguishes Andalucians from other Spaniards. Moorish influence can be seen in people's features, their behaviour and the style of their *pueblos* (villages). In AD756, Abderraman I established himself as emir in Córdoba. Jews

Growing evidence shows that early man lived in the area of Nerja

and Christians were permitted their faiths on payment of taxes. Christians who did not convert to Islam were known as *Mozárabes*; those who did were *Muladies* or *Renegados*. Abderraman III raised himself to the status of caliph in 929 and consolidated Muslim rule in the peninsula. Córdoba became Western Europe's most advanced and cultured city. Almansur, a military strongman during the reign of weak Hisham II, conducted *aceifas* (campaigns) against slowly strengthening Christian kingdoms in the north of the peninsula. When he died in 1002 the caliphate

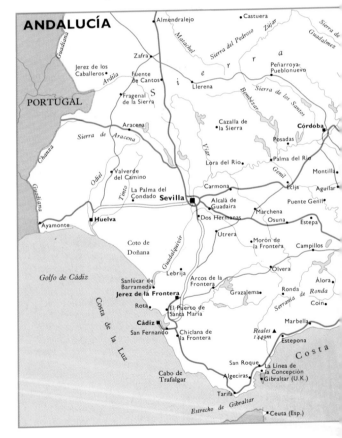

began its decline. Hisham III, last caliph, abdicated in 1031, and Muslim Spain split into 26 *taifas* (small kingdoms). Some warred with each other, some made pacts with Christian rulers in the north, and others consolidated. The strongest were the kingdoms of Seville and Granada, the latter incorporating Málaga and most of the coast. Certain *taifas* called for help from the Almoravid emir in North Africa, and from 1090, the Almoravides began uniting them and imposing a strict religious order which included the persecution of Christians and Jews. Their rivals in North Africa, the

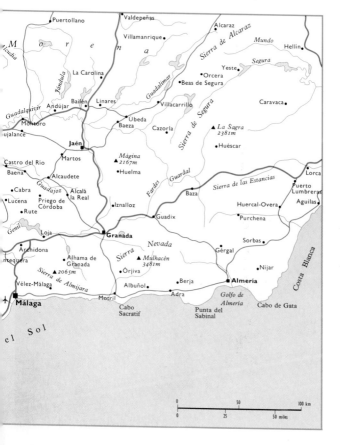

Almohades, arrived in Al Andalus in 1147 and by 1170 had replaced the Almoravides. They improved the economy and were keen builders, and initially they offered religious freedom. After their defeat in 1212 by Ferdinand III of Castile at the battle of Las Navas de Tolosa, the Muslims were again split.

Christian Reconquest

The Christian Reconquest of Spain was well on its way by this time, but the kingdom of Granada, including Málaga, held out. Conquered territory was divided among the nobility, church and military orders which created the *latifundios* (large estates) and ruling families whose existence was to cause so much socio-economic damage in the region, right up to the present time. Muslims remaining in Christian territories were known as *Mudéjares*; those who converted were called *Moriscos*. Mudéjar craftsmen were employed by Christians, and developed a distinct architectural style which is named after them. Jews were forced to live in *Juderías* (enclosed

Stone Age dolmen at Conjunto Dolmenico, Antequera

The Roman legacy in Spain is as much cultural as it is architectural

city districts). Ferdinand II of Aragón and Isabel I of Castile, *los Reyes Católicos* (the Catholic Monarchs), who married in 1469, had their campaign against the Muslims blessed by the Pope as a Holy Crusade, and they instituted the ruthless Inquisition to root out heretics. By 1490 they had conquered most of Granada's territory. On 2 January 1492, King Boabdil of Granada gave them the keys of his city. They had promised him that his people could live peacefully practising their beliefs and customs. It was not a promise they kept.

In 1493 Cristobal Colón (Christopher Columbus) returned to Spain with news that he had reached the New World. Spain started hauling back the treasures of the vast areas it conquered, and Seville grew rich as the world's busiest port. Grand Renaissance buildings were commissioned in cities and towns in an extravagant display of wealth. With the subjugation of Muslims and then the final expulsion of Moriscos (1609), Andalucía's productiveness progressively declined. Many people also left to settle in the New World. The decline was general in Spain, though it was not obvious at the time.

Fishing villages are now holiday resorts but the old skills are still practised

Fall of the Empire

During the following century Spain weakened politically but culture flourished. Architecture blossomed into the baroque style, and Andalucía produced the great artists Diego Velázquez, Bartolomé Murillo and Alonso Cano, among a host of others.

The 18th century started and ended with wars, culminating in the early 1800s with the Peninsular War against Napoleon's forces. They had a policy of destroying or looting architectural and artistic treasures, and this caused great losses in Andalucía.

The 19th century was marked by continuous political upheaval, and by 1898 Spain had lost all of its colonial empire after its war with the United States. Movements for agrarian reform in Andalucía were usually ruthlessly suppressed. Political confusion and economic stagnation continued into the 20th century. With the support of King Alfonso XIII, the dictator General Primo de Rivera ran the country between 1923 and 1930, but then resigned. The

king left Spain in 1931. Andalucía strongly supported the socialists who won the elections of 1931, but again the country could not pull itself out of political chaos. In July 1936, army factions, so-called Nationalists later led by General Franco, rose against the Popular Front government. The ensuing Civil War lasted until early 1939, and each village, town and city has its sad and separate story of the horrors. Franco, *el Caudillo* ('the Leader'), ran Spain until his death in 1975. Andalucía was not his favourite place and the region received little benevolence from a man who saw himself as a kind father of the people.

Since Franco's death, King Juan Carlos I has helped nurture the country peacefully back to democracy. The open, cultured and sports-loving royal family – the king, Queen Sofia, two princesses and the crown prince Felipe – is widely popular. Felipe González, President of the Government (Prime Minister) since 1983, comes from Seville where he first began his clandestine support and work for the PSOE (Socialist Party) during the dark Franco years.

A donkey taxi dressed up with Andalucian flair

Andalucía Today

People from other parts of Spain complain that
the prominence of Andalucians in Madrid's
corridors of power favours the region. Many
Andalucians complain that they suffer because
the central government is afraid to show them
any favouritism. They have their own regional
government in Seville, the Junta de Andalucía,
also securely socialist, against whom the
region's agricultural workers are constantly
doing battle. They complain of poor payment
and treatment by the landowners. Emptying
villages and deserted *cortijos* (countryside
houses) testify to the exodus from the land to
the developed coastal strip and to cities within
Andalucía and beyond, in search of work or
retirement after a life of toil. The service
industries, especially tourism, are the principal
source of people's earnings. A chill wind began
blowing through the tourism sector in 1989,
freezing out many businesses, but the region
seems to have weathered the storm.

The drop was largely at the budget end of the
market with the worst effects on the hotel
industry servicing the package holiday
operators. The drop in numbers of passengers
passing through Málaga airport was less
dramatic, because residential tourism remained
strong. People owning their villas and
apartments or regularly renting privately are of
the greatest significance along the Costa del
Sol. More than 100,000 foreigners, mainly
British, German, Dutch and Scandinavian, live
in Málaga province, and 90 per cent of coastal
real estate developments are bought by
foreigners, more than half by Britons. At first
most of the blame for the tourism crisis was put
on the economic conditions prevailing in
Britain, which also provides the largest number
of visitors on organised packages. Later the
tourist industry and authorities realised that it
was up to them to make changes. The main aim
has been to attract 'quality tourism', to upgrade
amenities and to promote the 'Costa del Golf' as
well as many other excellent sports facilities.
Around 30 golf courses are available and by
1995 there may be 40. Twelve marinas in
Málaga province serve sailing and boating
enthusiasts, and tennis courts are plentiful.

Villages are trying to stem the flow of young blood to the coast

Another important change has been to identify the Costa del Sol more closely with the rest of Andalucía. Today the coast is promoted as a well-serviced residential belt with easy access to the region's fascinating interior and its monumental cities and towns.

The landscape is indeed very beautiful and varied, even just a few miles inland from the narrow coastal plain. High mountains, folding hills, often terraced, and deep valleys contrast with the wide and intensively farmed plain of the Río Guadalquivir beyond. Time stands still in whitewashed pueblos dripping down hillsides and spurs or hidden in valleys. Nature reserves and parks cover 17 per cent of Andalucian territory. In Málaga province, El Torcal's lunar landscape contrasts with Cádiz province's thickly wooded Sierra de Grazalema, and there are many more areas to enchant the nature lover. For people prepared to leave the

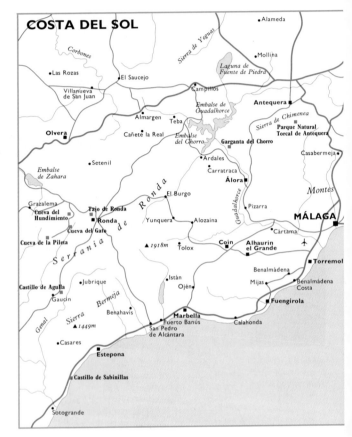

beaches and bar stools, there is an enormous amount to see and do, as well as every opportunity for sports. Last but not least, Andalucía offers many chances for socialising with the Andaluz people at their popular fiestas and *ferias* (fairs). A new awareness of their cultural identity has caused revitalising of old-established celebrations and the creation of new ones. Flamenco has its origins among persecuted minorities in the mountains of Andalucía. Today, the whole of Spain has taken up dancing the *sevillana*, a lighter, modern derivative.

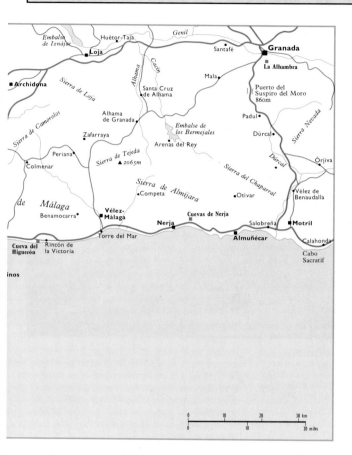

1992 and Beyond

Much has already been done to improve the
infrastructure along the coast by widening and
rebuilding the main N340 coastal highway,
building town bypasses, sewage and
wastewater treatment plants, and regenerating
beaches. In regard to stopping pollution of the
Mediterranean, Málaga province claims to be
doing more than anywhere else along this
threatened sea's coastline. Málaga's airport is
being greatly improved, mainly by the building
of a new international terminal to service 11
million passengers a year, the projected

BACKGROUND

Andalucía plans to move out of the shade and find its place in the sun by the year 2000

number for the year 2000. The city's railway station is also being renovated. More needs to be done for infrastructural improvement, and most of it is envisaged in the massive regional development project, 'Plan Andalucía 92' or in provincial and municipal initiatives. A four-lane toll expressway stretching 32 miles (51km) from Málaga to Estepona is planned. East of the city, an expressway from Rincón de la Victoria to Nerja is on the drawing board. Throughout Málaga province and much of Andalucía, roads are being improved. Health services in the province are improving too, with the opening of the Hospital Clínico in the city and the building of a hospital near Marbella. First aid centres along the coast have been or will be upgraded. By the year 2000, Andalucía should be very different. It is likely that the rest of the Costa del Sol will have moved upmarket to emulate Marbella, its most glittering star, which attracts the rich and famous, including (it is said) some very dubious characters.

MÁLAGA

During Phoenician times Malaca, as it was then known, was the second most important trading port in Spain, with a valuable fish-salting industry from which is derived its name (*malac* means 'to salt'). The Romans created a thriving colony, rich from the good farmland and inland silver mines. The Moors transformed Málaga into the principal port of the kingdom of Granada and heavily fortified the seafront and town centre. According to contemporary Moorish writers, 'this paradise on earth' was a vital trading centre, busy, populated and extremely beautiful. Some of the local products, especially figs, received acclaim as far abroad as India and China. During the Christian Reconquest, the city was beseiged for more than three and a half months, finally surrendering on 18 August 1487. The ensuing repopulation by Christian immigrants from the north created economic mismanagement and hastened a decline which has lasted until quite recently.

During the last century, Málaga became a popular residence for foreigners, particularly the English, and many wintered here for its therapeutic climate. Today the city of over half a million people is still very much Andalucian in character. It offers a welcome respite for visitors from northern Europe, but is often overlooked. People tend to use it as a stopover on their way to one of the many nearby beach resorts, or as an excursion destination.

Inland, the protective mountain ranges stave off the northern winds, giving Málaga one of the most even climates in all of Europe. Nearby vineyards produce grapes for the popular local wines, and the surrounding landscape is dotted with citrus orchards and vegetable plots. The city's river is Río Guadalmedina, which

Castillo de Gibralfaro stands above the garden fortress of the Alcazaba

MÁLAGA

only flows sporadically, but splits Málaga in two. Eastwards lie the narrow and crowded back streets of the old part of town; to the west, a modern expansion of urban development marches virtually unabated as far as Fuengirola. As provincial capital of the Costa del Sol's tourist resorts, and with its attractive harbour and good communications, Málaga is the most important southern coastal city after Cádiz. Bustling *alamedas* (walkways) and congested back streets make it quite hectic, especially during the summer months. Crowds are one of the penalties for being such a rapidly expanding centre of tourism and commerce on Spain's hottest coastline. Off season, or at least out of business hours, it is simpler to enjoy a city that may be poorly endowed by national standards but is rich in a variety of ways and full of character.

The face and layout of Málaga is changing as projects within the 'Plan Andalucía 92' and local initiatives come into effect. Regeneration of El Palo beach has included the building of a new promenade. On the east side, regeneration has included the creation of a long new beach, from the Levante dike to El Morlaco, a new promenade and a landscape of palm trees and gardens, linked to a new park.

Remodelling and consolidation of the Alcazaba, Gibralfaro and Roman theatre has brought a new street layout in the area and the creation of a botanical garden. La Coracha, a row of

old houses on the hill facing the sea, is being remodelled into a cultural and tourist complex, and buildings in the city centre are being renovated. El Retiro will be an ornithological park of 40 acres (16 hectares) with 2,000 birds of 250 species. Piers One and Two of the harbour are being developed as public sports amenities, and the mouth of the Guadalmedina river is being enhanced. Research companies and others are being attracted to the new Technological Park on the site of 420 acres (170 hectares) near Campanillas in the northwest of the city.

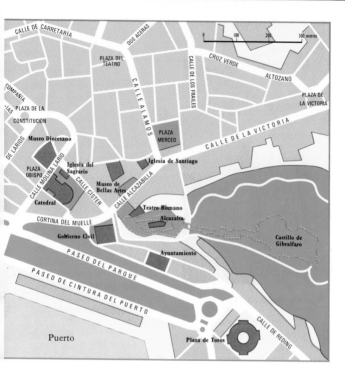

Horse Taxis

For those with thin shoes or suffering from the summer heat, the best and most relaxed way to get to know the city centre and prominent sights is by Málaga's own local horsedrawn taxi service.

There are a number of starting points, including the Paseo del Parque, Plaza de Toros and the train station. The best times to avoid the overwhelming traffic snarls are on Sundays or during the daily lunchbreak, between 14.00 and 17.00 hrs. Agree on the price before accepting the ride, in order to avoid problems afterwards.

WHAT TO SEE

The majority of places of interest lie within a short distance of each other around the old town centre. At the end of this section there are a couple of suggested walks around this part of the city. Málaga, unfortunately, has the usual city problem of street crime.

◆◆◆
ALCAZABA

The elaborate fortress with its numerous patios, fountains and gardens surrounds a former palace, and was constructed during the mid-11th century on

Tranquillity at the Alcazaba

Roman foundations. Claims that it is the most important Moorish military construction in the country are based more on its unique defence network rather than on any obvious attributes. During the 18th century it was abandoned until its rather over-enthusiastic restoration in 1933. The palace area now houses a small but interesting museum with assorted collections from the local past, including Roman statues and some fine examples of Moorish ceramics. There is also a large-scale model of the Alcazaba as it used to be. Outside the main entrance you will notice the remains of a **Roman amphitheatre**, quite recently discovered. It was probably from here that the marble columns were salvaged to construct the curious Puerta de las Columnas (Gate of Columns) within the fortress precincts.

Open: (winter) 10.00–13.00 hrs and 16.00–19.00 hrs; (summer) 11.00–13.00 hrs and 17.00–20.00 hrs; (Sundays all year) 10.00–14.00 hrs.

◆◆
CASTILLO DE GIBRALFARO
This is best reached by horse taxi or, more energetically, by a steep climb through gardens to one side of the Alcazaba – but beware, the path is a blackspot for muggings.
Constructed during the early 14th century, the castle is joined by parallel ramparts to the Alcazaba below. It occupies the site of earlier Phoenician fortifications and a lighthouse from which it got its name (*gebel-faro* meaning mountain of the lighthouse).
From the panoramic view of the city and port, you can pick out some of the key features of the town centre. Almost immediately below is a bird's-eye view of the bullring, while beyond, towards the port, lies the popular restaurant area of La Malagueta. The oasis of palm trees that runs parallel to the dockfront shades the Paseo del Parque and its adjacent gardens. Slightly to the left of the Alcazaba, you cannot miss the imposing town hall, and beyond that stands the distinctive single tower of the cathedral. Still further away, and only viewed as rooftops, sprawls the oldest part of town and hub of daily pedestrian activity.
Open: May be under restoration: check locally.

◆◆
CATEDRAL
Calle Molina Lario
Travel writers and historians have mostly described this building in harsh terms, and at the turn of this century one guidebook went so far as to call it an 'unmeaning pile, characterised by all the defects of the pseudo-classical school at the worst periods'. But try not to be too put off, it does have a couple of saving graces. Construction was started in 1528 by the eminent architect Diego de Siloé, but was stopped due to lack of funds shortly afterwards. The building was partly destroyed in 1680 by an earthquake, and work was resumed again in 1719 with modifications, stopped once more in 1765 and then never finished. Its two towers, one of which rises no further than the second storey, have prompted its nickname of La Manquita – the Cripple – and for seven months during the Civil War it was occupied by Republican forces who murdered the priests and ransacked its treasures. Clearly this unfortunate edifice was never destined for a glorious history. By far the most exciting feature is its choir, the principal reason for a visit. The stalls were designed by Luis Ortiz and the Italian sculptor Giuseppe Michael, but the 40 superbly crafted statues of saints were completed by the Granadan sculptor, Pedro de Mena, in 1662. In the Capilla de los Reyes, reconstructed after the Civil War, stands a figure of the Virgin supposedly carried into battle by Ferdinand during the Christian Reconquest. Other chapels exhibit paintings and statues by Pedro de Mena and his great tutor, Alonso Cano. *Open:* 10.00–13.00 hrs and 16.00–17.30 hrs.

◆◆◆
MUSEO DE ARTES POPULARES
Pasillo de Santa Isabel 7
This is a great opportunity for visitors of all ages to wander through a fascinating collection of ordinary and extraordinary objects from everyday life in the past – tools, carts, dolls, ceramics, posters and more. As a bonus the museum is housed

The verdant Museo de Artes Populares

in a delightful 17th-century building, once a *posada* (inn). *Open:* (summer) 10.00–13.00 hrs and 17.00–20.00 hrs; (winter) 10.00–13.00 hrs and 16.00–19.00 hrs; (Sundays all year) 10.00–14.00 hrs.

◆◆
MUSEO DE BELLAS ARTES
Calle San Agustín 6
Dedicated mostly to Spanish artists, the museum has interesting selections of paintings by Murillo, Alonso Cano, Ribera and Pedro de Mena. Upstairs are some early sketches by Picasso as a boy – he was born in Málaga – along with paintings by his master, Muñoz Degrain. The building, a 16th-century mansion, also contains some fine Roman mosaics from nearby Cártama in a patio close to the entrance. *Open:* (summer) 10.00–13.00 hrs and 17.00–20.00 hrs; (winter) 10.00–13.00 hrs and 16.00–19.00 hrs; (Sundays all year) 10.00–14.00 hrs. Closed Monday.

◆
MUSEO DIOCESANO
Plaza Obispo
A large and slightly overpowering collection of religious works, from madonnas to woodcuts is displayed here. The baroque building used to be the episcopal palace. *Open:* 09.00–13.00 hrs and 16.00–19.00 hrs.

◆
PLAZA DE TOROS
Calle Maestranza
Built in 1874, the large but otherwise unremarkable bullring does permit visitors to wander through the 'nether

Málaga's ill-fated cathedral

regions' of bull pens, butcher shop and bullfighters' chapel. There is also a tiny museum.

Walks in Málaga
Two simple walks will allow you to see most places of interest around the city centre, including the principal shopping precincts and markets. For both it is convenient to start off in the Plaza de la Marina at the western end of the Paseo del Parque and above the large underground carpark. As a taster for either route, you may like to descend first into the carpark to glimpse the remains of the Moorish city walls that were discovered during construction and have been partially preserved. Places in **bold** are described as individual entries.

WALK 1: OLD MÁLAGA

Start at the Plaza de la Marina. Heading across the road, you enter Calle Molina Lario beside the Hotel Málaga Palacio, and shortly arrive at the **Catedral**. A little further, on the opposite side of the road in the Plaza Obispo, stands the episcopal palace housing the **Museo Diocesano**. Turn right down the Calle Císter, and almost immediately on your right is the original Gothic entrance to the Iglesia del Sagrario. Built in 1488 on the site of the grand mosque, the church was reconstructed almost totally in the 18th century. The portal is the only surviving part of the original edifice.

Opposite the church, the Calle San Agustín leads you to the **Museo de Bellas Artes**. After forking right a little further, you will see the Iglesia de Santiago. Another 15th-century construction, also rebuilt in the 18th century, it has an interesting Mudéjar tower and original entrance. Picasso was baptised in the church, and his birthplace lies just around the corner in the Plaza Merced. Before going there, take a short detour down the narrow Calle Tomás de Cozar, opposite the church, an atmospheric back street of secluded patios and Moorish origins that leads to the Calle de Beatas. Turning right, you continue past wealthy town houses of the last century for four blocks until arriving at the Plaza del Teatro. You can turn right here (or earlier if you like) and then double back along the Calle Alamos, former northern boundary of the walled town, to the Plaza Merced.

In the centre of the plaza stands an obelisk in remembrance of General Torrijos and 50 other liberals who were shot after the War of Independence. In one corner a small plaque reminds you that Picasso was born here. There is also a tourist information office.

Next stop is a well-deserved refreshment in one of the bars along the Calle Alcazabilla, beneath the walls of the fortress. Revitalised, you may by now be ready for a little climbing. But first have a quick look at the Roman amphitheatre before entering the **Alcazaba**, which is constructed on Roman foundations.

On leaving the Alcazaba, you can turn immediately left and follow a winding path through gardens to the top of the hill and the **Castillo de Gibralfaro**. Unfortunately this path has a reputation for attracting muggers, so use it with caution. The alternative is to stay at street level and continue your wander beneath the orange and cypress trees of the Jardines de Puerta Oscura until you reach the large roundabout at the eastern end of the Paseo del Parque. On the far side, behind the hospital, is the **Plaza de Toros**. To return along the Paseo del Parque to the Plaza de la Marina, make sure you are on the southern side so that you can wander through the shaded gardens of the park, and enjoy some of the 2,000 different species of trees and flowers, maybe stopping for a rest at one of the cafés.

MÁLAGA

WALK 2: THROUGH THE SIDE STREETS

Starting at the Plaza de la Marina, cross the road and take the Calle Marqués de Larios northwards off the Alameda Principal. This street was only built during the last century as a modern access into the old town. Near the far end, on the right, lies a tourist information office. From here, much of the route depends on your nose and sense of direction, since you can follow any one of the dozens of side streets and small alleyways leading to the left or right. But perhaps the best way is first to follow the route which encompasses most of the interesting side streets and then, once orientated, to wander at will.

The top of the Calle Marqués de Larios opens into the small Plaza de la Constitución, where you turn left and head straight down Calle Especerías. A short detour to the left down Calle San Juan will lead you to the Iglesia de San Juan, an 18th-century restoration of one of the oldest churches in Málaga. Go back to Calle Especerías and continue along Calle Cisneros to the river. Immediately to the left is the **Museo de Artes Populares**. Follow the river for a short while, then fork left down Calle Arriola until you come to the huge city market of Atarazanas, bursting with life and filled with every imaginable fruit and vegetable. After a wander through the stalls, try and leave by the southern gateway. This is the Puerta de Atarazanas, the original Moorish entrance to

what was an 11th-century naval warehouse. From here it is only a few metres to the Alameda Principal, where you are within sight of your starting point.

Accommodation

When Málaga's dormitory town, Torremolinos, gained local autonomy, the provincial capital was left with only a few hotels to its name. For a vast choice, see Torremolinos.

Bahía Málaga, 3-star, Calle Somera 8 (tel: 22 43 05). Friendly, well kept and close to the port. One great advantage is the private parking. 44 rooms.

Don Curro, 3-star, Calle Sancha de Lara 7 (tel: 22 72 00). Just off the Alameda Principal and close to the cathedral, the hotel is convenient for shopping and sightseeing. The 105 rooms are smart and surprisingly peaceful considering the hotel also accommodates a popular bingo hall.

Las Vegas, 3-star, Paseo de Sancha 22 (tel: 21 77 12). Large, though dated, edifice within 10 minutes walk of the centre. Principal attractions are its tropical garden and swimming pool. 68 rooms and five suites.

Málaga Palacio, 3-star, Calle Cortina del Muelle 1 (tel: 21 51 85). Grandiose and polished atmosphere in traditional Malaguenian style. The hotel is professionally run and trim, with good views of city and port from upper rooms and top floor café. Swimming pool and sun terrace on the roof. The 220 rooms are the most expensive in town.

Parador de Gibralfaro, 3-star (tel: 22 19 02). Perched high above the city and close to the castle, this small parador is quiet with an intimate atmosphere. The design is regional and the views are superb, though reflected in the prices.

Lis, 2-star, Calle Córdoba 7 (tel: 22 73 00). Standard 2-star comfort at reasonable prices. 53 rooms, some of them apartments.

Venecia, 2-star, Alameda Principal 9 (tel: 21 36 36). Right at the heart of everything with basic comforts. 40 rooms.

Niza, 1-star, Calle Larios 2 (tel: 22 77 04). Simple but well kept, on the town's main shopping street. 53 rooms.

Nightlife

As you might expect in a big, energetic city, Málaga offers plenty of opportunities to while away the midnight hours, be it in a discothèque, music pub or piano bar. Live flamenco, jazz or rock shows are regularly staged, and for those in search of quieter entertainment, there are also frequent theatre, dance and classical music performances.

The recently restored **Teatro Cervantes**, Calle Ramón Marín (tel: 22 41 00), is Málaga's leading cultural venue. You may find theatre, opera or classical music on the programme. Check with the box office or tourist office for the latest details.

Most cinemas present only Spanish-dubbed films, but the **Cine Club Universitario**, Calle San Agustín, offers original versions, usually in English, on Tuesdays and Thursdays. Relaxing bars that leave room

Fiesta makes an exhibition of itself

for conversation include the downbeat **El Cantor de Jazz**, Calle Lazcano 7, the more modern **Carlos Gorospe**, Calle Pintor Sorolla 11, with occasional art exhibitions, and the comfortable **La Casa del Conde**, Calle Santa Lucía 9, where you are likely to find some live music.

A more upbeat atmosphere and livelier crowds can be found at a handful of bars around the Plaza Mitjana, including **Tita Conchi**, **Down Town** and **Boom Beer**. In the area of the cathedral and Alcazaba, the crowds circulate between the small **Café Teatro**, Calle Afligidos 5, **Arriba va**, Calle Mundo Nuevo 34, and **Catedral**, Calle Cister 4. A taxi-ride away near El Corte Inglés is **La Medina**, Calle Compositor

Lehmberg Ruiz 32, a café by day and highly fashionable, ultra-modern music bar by night.

La Malagueta buzzes with music and dance most evenings. If you can find space, pop into **Ragtime**, Paseo de Reding 12. If live flamenco is more your taste, you can choose from **Gloria Bendita**, Avenida Cánovas del Castillo, **Terrá** or **Anea**. **H20**, Calle Fernando Camino, is a nearby disco club.

If you want to party until dawn, you will have to move on later to the hectically youthful Pedregalejo district. Dozens of bars and discothèques attract the city's liveliest elements, to such names as **Duna**, Avenida Juan Sebastián Elcano, **Wizz**, Calle Bolivia, or **La Chancla**, on the beach.

Restaurants

Although Málaga is of obvious tourist interest, the city does not go out of its way to cater for

Civic glory: Málaga city hall

visitors, and most eating places are run by Malaguenians for Malaguenians. Menus are predominantly regional, with heavy emphasis on fish and shellfish, and cooking standards are generally high. Foreign cuisine is only slowly gaining popularity, and visitors are unlikely to find more than Chinese or Italian alternatives to the local diet.

Fritura malagueña is the city's culinary pride and joy, a plate of mixed fried fish usually composed of anchovies, sardines, *calamares* (squid), red mullet and small fry. When fresh, it is delicious.

Pescaderías and *marisquerías* (seafood restaurants) offer huge varieties of fish and shellfish dishes, often by weight. Prices can be quite high.

Town Centre

There are dozens of restaurants, snack bars, marisquerías and small taverns to choose from. For a light meal or tapa and a glass of wine, you need look no

further than Calle Marín García, which is packed with eateries. **El Boquerón de Plata** is best for seafood, especially prawns. Manchego cheeses and *jamón serrano* (ham) are specialities of **La Manchega** and **Lo Güeno**, or if you prefer a good choice of sherries with your ham, look in at **La Tasca**. More seafood is served at **Casa Vicente** (Calle Comisario), and at **Antigua Casa Guardia** (Alameda Principal 18), where the large selection of draught wines is served in an atmosphere that has changed little during the last 150 years of business.

If you want a more complete menu, then search out:

Café de la Opera, Teatro Cervantes, Calle Ramón Marín 3 (tel: 22 38 78). Housed in Málaga's leading theatre, the Andalucian dishes are imaginative and well presented. Medium prices, closed Sunday night and Monday.

La Espuela, Calle Trinidad Grund 14 (tel: 21 71 82). Solid home cooking in a traditional Andalucian atmosphere. Closed Sundays.

Rincón de Mata, Calle Esparteros 8 (tel: 22 31 35). Once again seafood is the speciality, and at reasonable prices. Try the shellfish soup or fresh sole.

La Malagueta

This area contains most of the city's best restaurants as well as numerous bars. Many people look no further, particularly for an evening meal. It comprises the streets between the bullring and the seafront on either side of the main road.

Antonio Martín, Paseo Marítimo (tel: 22 21 13) has been the leader of Málaga's restaurant community for more than a century. Perfectly located on the seafront, with a large terrace, it predictably specialises in seafood. Prices are high.

Café de Paris, Calle Vélez Málaga (tel: 22 50 43). Elegant, upmarket restaurant serving international dishes with a strong French influence. Try the green peppers stuffed with cod or the pheasant in cream sauce. Expensive but good value. Closed Tuesdays.

Dragon de Oro, Avenida Cánovas del Castillo 3 (tel: 22 74 87). Chinese food at reasonable prices.

El Figón de Bonilla, Calle Cervantes (tel; 22 32 23). Fish, along with some delicious local dishes. Try any of the stews or the oxtail. Closed Sundays.

La Taberna del Pintor, Calle Maestranza 6 (tel: 22 53 15). Specialities are the charcoal-cooked meats, served in a relaxed ambience. Very popular with the younger crowd, both for quality and economy. All of the meats are good, and some are sold by weight. Closed Sundays.

Trastevere, Avenida Cánovas del Castillo 10. Italian trattoria with all the old favourites at moderate prices.

Pedregalejo and El Palo

These two eastern city suburbs lie on the beach, about one-and-a-half miles (2.5km) from the town centre. Fresh fish within sight of the waves is the order of the day, with a large selection of restaurants to choose from. In

Pedregalejo, you should investigate **Los Amigos** and **El Lirio**, both on the Paseo Marítimo, or **El Cabra** (Calle del Copo 21). In El Palo, **Tintero II** (Playa del Chanquete) offers a similar seafood menu, with some rice specialities. Memorable places include:

Casa Pedro, Paseo Marítimo, El Palo (tel: 29 00 13). One of the oldest and most popular restaurants of the area. Its huge dining room can get very crowded in summer. Try the *paella especial*, grilled sardines or *fritura malagueña*. Closed Monday nights.

Refectorium, Avenida Juan Sebastián Elcano 146, El Palo (tel: 29 45 93). Meat rather than fish is the principal ingredient on the menu and can be enjoyed in a variety of home-cooked dishes, typical of the south. Traditional atmosphere, though prices are high. Closed Mondays.

Shopping

The best and busiest shopping area is to the north side of the Alameda Principal in the old town, although certain interesting shops lie towards the port. Since daily trade is almost exclusively aimed at the local inhabitants, you will not find a typical selection of souvenirs or tourist goods, and prices are normally moderate. The most distinctive local handicrafts are the ceramic figurines known as *barros malagueños*. These typically portray bullfighters, dancers, smugglers and fishermen. Tooled leatherwork, marquetry and brass items can also be found.

Heading across the bridge from the Alameda Principal, you are likely to pass a number of street stalls selling jewellery, souvenirs and nick-nacks. Prices here are very good. A little further on the right you will arrive at Málaga's shoppers' paradise, the huge El Corte Inglés department store, principal attraction for most visitors on a buying spree. It is also recommended as a place to park. Everything from keyrings to dining room suites can be bought here, though prices for everyday articles can be steep. The top floor has an excellent cafeteria and restaurant, serving snacks, mixed dishes and set meals (very busy at lunchtimes). The store is open all day, Monday to Saturday.

Special Events

Málaga is a city of tradition, and traditionally the people of Málaga love their fiestas. There are few places in the country where the spirit and energy of a society is expressed in such an exuberant and vivacious manner. Even Holy Week (before Easter), normally a sombre occasion, becomes a dramatic spectacle with the Malaguenians, and visitors are more than welcome.

Carnival (leading up to Shrove Tuesday in February/March) is very popular with singing, dancing and parades. Málaga's **Holy Week** is one of the finest in Spain, with 33 *cofradías*, or brotherhoods, putting on continuous processions throughout the week. They form arguably one of the most serious and grandiose displays of religious devotion in Europe. Streets are packed day and night to watch the monumental floats, some weighing up to six tonnes and carried by 100 men. During the **Cruces de Mayo** (beginning of May) the city is adorned with floral crosses. **San Juan** (23 June) sees the burning of satirical images on bonfires at midnight, plus dancing and events on the Paseo Marítimo. There are traditional religious processions during **Corpus Christi** (May/June). The maritime processions of the **Virgen del Carmen** (16 July) are common to most of the coast, and end with fireworks. The largest annual event is the **Feria de Agosto** (August), including fairs, processions, flamenco, *verdiales* (folk groups unique to Andalucía), exhibitions, a food week (local menus are served specially in certain restaurants), bullfights, fireworks, and a huge barbecue on El Palo beach on the last night. At the end of August, the **Fiesta de la Vendimia** celebrates the local wine harvest. Finally the **Fiesta de Verdiales** (on 28 December) is a music festival with competitions held in the hills near the city.

Old and new blend in the city centre

LA AXARQUÍA

The Axarquía region can loosely be described as the southeastern corner of Málaga province. Its border follows the coast from Málaga city to Maro, just beyond Nerja, and turns inland to make a rough semicircle along the mountain ridges of the *sierras* Alhama, Tejeda and Almijara, and back down to the coast at Maro.

The area comprises more than 30 different towns and villages that occupy the fertile coast and broad inland valley of the Río de Vélez and its adjacent mountain slopes. Caves and natural springs pocket the northeastern hillsides of the Axarquía, part of which has been designated as the park of Sierra del Alcázar. Unirrigated agriculture still constitutes the backbone of the hillside economies, while in the valley lowlands the multi-crop market gardens are supplied by a large reservoir near Viñuela. Coastal populations, while still retaining some of the tradition and function of fishing communities, are mostly preoccupied with the development of the tourist trade and its allied services.

Origins

Palaeolithic people were the first to take advantage of the area's natural riches and mild climate. Finds in the caves of Nerja and Rincón de la Victoria bear witness to the social development and hunting prowess of more than 20,000 years ago. But it was not until the arrival of the seafaring Phoenicians (approximately 1000BC) that small trading settlements were established along the shoreline and lower foothills of the Axarquía, as collection points for metals mined high in the *sierras* and a variety of fish products. Greek, Carthaginian and Roman colonisers controlled the local commerce at different times, but it was the Greeks who established the most significant colony. This was Mainake, founded in 700BC, probably close to where Vélez-Málaga stands today, which introduced the olive and vine to the region's agriculture.

The Moorish invasion of the peninsula heralded the next dramatic step in the evolution of the Axarquía, and the region owes much of its present character to seven centuries of Islamic influence on commerce, irrigation and culture. Its sheltered and fertile alluvial plains became prime production areas for grapes, olives, cereals, silk and sugar cane – most of which are still being cultivated today – and the majority of small rural communities in the area started life as prosperous Moorish farming estates.

During the Christian Reconquest, the Axarquía was the scene of an overwhelming Moorish victory over Christian forces (1483). Although the Moors were finally defeated in 1487, it is clear from the remains of fortifications in almost every village that the victors paid a high price. Nor did the conflict finish then. Religious intolerance and repression sparked the Moorish Rebellion of the Alpujarras in 1568, which

Balcón de Europa: Mediterranean views and a continental atmosphere

spread like wildfire through the Axarquía. After subduing Vélez-Málaga, Christian forces shifted their attention to Frigiliana which became the final bloody battleground. This was quickly followed by almost total expulsion of all Moors who had not converted to Christianity, and the villages of the Axarquía were repopulated by immigrants from the north who knew little of the local economy. The result was a gradual decline in prosperity that was hastened by plague and pestilence, and continued well into this century.

The Modern Axarquía

Today, the Axarquía wears two faces. Mass development of the 1970s and 1980s has erased most vestiges of the past from along the coast and replaced them with modern tourist developments. Go only a few kilometres inland however, and you will find that little has changed. Sugar cane fields still cloak the flatlands, though these are now bordered by rapidly

expanding orchards of avocado and *chirimoya* (custard apple). The dryer hillsides continue to bear important crops of grapes and olives as they have for thousands of years. Plastic-roofed market gardens also dot the countryside, and can yield as many as three vegetable crops a year.

Typical villages of the area have winding back streets that twist between whitewashed houses, some clearly Moorish in origin with courtyard patios and arched passageways. As every town had its fortification, so did it have its church. Most were built immediately after the Christian Reconquest, and some contain interesting Mudéjar architecture.

The local inhabitants are relaxed and friendly, and they are always welcoming; but your best opportunity to experience the Axarquian hospitality and culture is during one of the local fiestas.

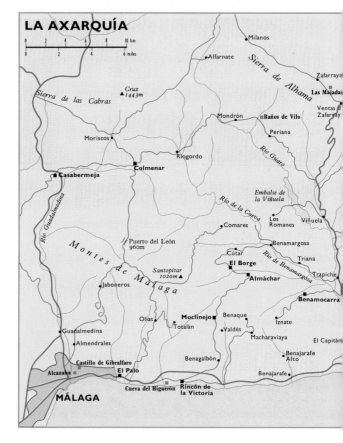

LA AXARQUÍA – COAST

WHAT TO SEE

◆◆◆
MARO

This charming and completely
unspoilt village lies about two
and a half miles (4km) east of
Nerja, close to the caves. It has
a wonderful setting, perched
high above the water and with
magnificent views of the coast,
all enhanced by utter
tranquillity. Steeply terraced
hillsides continue to produce an
abundance of crops, much as
they have since the Romans first
established a small community
here almost 2,000 years ago,
and there is a marked absence
of modern villas and tourist
urbanisations. Since there are
virtually no shops, you will find

Relaxing under Maro's shady palms

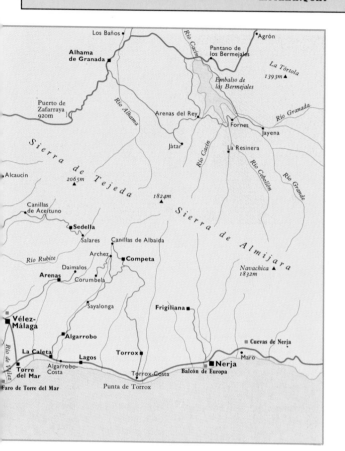

Nerja – tumbling towards the cliffs

none of the usual hustle and bustle. There may be traffic jams when too many cars try to reach the small but delightful beaches at the bottom of the cliffs.

Maro has not forgotten its historical role as a stopping off point for the weary (or curious) traveller who may be heading along the coast. A handful of restaurants serve regional menus in unpretentious surroundings, while two small hotels offer apartment and hotel facilities in good locations.

◆◆◆
NERJA

Perched on the brow of low sea cliffs, Nerja commands impressive panoramas of the coast in either direction. Below lie small coves and some excellent long sand beaches, very popular in summer and among the town's principal attractions. Inland, steep mountain slopes accommodate a burgeoning chalet population as they rise towards the distant peaks of the Sierra de Almijara.

Old aqueducts, stone-terraced market gardens and the occasional time-ravaged watchtower are reminders of the past.

By Mediterranean standards, however, Nerja is still quite young. Naricha, as it was then called, started life as a Moorish farming estate during the 10th century, centre of the silk and sugar industries for the area. For centuries it survived in delicate equilibrium as a small fishing and farming community. The advent of organised tourism during the 1970s changed all that, but in spite of the destructive effect that hordes of foreign visitors normally have on the local landscape, Nerja has still managed to retain its picturesque look and small-town atmosphere.

The area is especially popular as a residential holiday resort among the British. Most visitors own their apartments or chalets, and many have decided to settle permanently in the area.

A significant proportion of local businesses are also owned by foreigners.

Nerja has one of Spain's most intriguing national monuments. The **Cuevas de Nerja** (Caves of Nerja) were discovered accidentally in 1959 by schoolboys hunting for bats. The caves quickly became recognised as important proof that Cro-Magnon man lived in this area more than 20,000 years ago, and some of the finds from early excavations are on display just inside the entrance. Early paintings of goats, deer, horses and fish have been discovered in some of the upper galleries, but these are unfortunately closed to the public.

For sheer size and clever lighting there is little to beat the caves in Europe. They are sometimes described as 'nature's prehistoric cathedral', and it is easy to see why. Stone 'organ' pipes stretch upwards, there are small 'side chapels' protected by limestone 'railings', and deep 'crypts' beneath the rocks.

The first large chamber has been converted into a form of auditorium for the annual festival of music and dance held during the summer, with seating for more than 600 people.

Following the well-marked walkway you then pass through the Hall of Ghosts, named after what looks like a shroud-covered figure, standing on one side. From there you reach the last and biggest section of the caves – the Hall of Cataclysms, a massive chamber some 200 feet (60m) high, strewn with the remains of broken stalactites from some past geological catastrophe. Rising from among the debris is a massive and intricately shaped column, claimed to be the tallest stalagmite in the world. At the far end of the cave, high up in the rock, a red light indicates the entrance to another and even larger cave system not yet open to the public.

Temperatures within the caves are a steady 60°F (21°C) throughout the year, so there is no need to overdress. A regular bus service runs from the town and there are full restaurant and bar facilities. Those driving should follow signs from the main coast road, about two and a half miles (4km) east of Nerja and just before the small village of Maro. (*Open:* (summer) 09.30–21.00 hrs; (winter) 10.00–13.30 hrs and 16.00–19.00 hrs.)

Nerja's other natural attraction is the **Balcón de Europa** (Balcony of Europe), a rocky promontory named by King Alfonso XII on a visit in 1885. The name stuck, and the promontory has served as the focus and principal vantage point of the town ever since. From here you can enjoy spectacular views of the rocky coastline, relax over a coffee in one of the bars or wander down to the small fisherman's cove just beneath.

Accommodation

Visitors normally stay in apartments or rent one of the many villas on offer in the surrounding urbanisations, but hotel accommodation is rapidly increasing in quantity and quality, with more than 2,000 beds now available.

Monica, Playa de la Torrecilla
(tel: 52 11 00), 4-star. Modern
and spacious 234-room package
holiday hotel, right on the beach
and replete with wall-to-wall
marble. Owned by Bass Horizon
Hotels, it is very popular with
the British.

Parador de Nerja, Calle El
Tablazo (tel: 52 00 50), 4-star.
Wonderfully located hotel, built
in the traditional Andalucian
style. Spacious gardens afford
panoramic views of the sea and
coastline, while an outside lift
allows easy access down to
Burriana beach. 60 rooms.

Balcón de Europa, Paseo Balcón
de Europa (tel: 52 08 00), 3-star.
Centrally located on the
seafront, close to shopping
areas and facing on to a small
beach. It has 105 rooms and 20
suites.

Marinas de Nerja, Carretera
Nacional 340 (tel: 52 22 00),
3-star. A modern and stylish
complex lying less than two
miles (3.2km) west of town,
beside the beach. One- and
two-bedroomed apartments are
available, along with
comprehensive sports and
entertainment facilities.

Perla Marina, Calle Mérida 7
(tel: 52 05 00), 3-star. New,
smart and right on the shore.
Its 104 rooms and four suites
are comfortable and well
serviced.

Nightlife
Summer evening entertainment
is comprehensive and lively.
Wander around the side streets
to the west of Avenida Castilla
Pérez (such as Calle Antonio
Millón or Calle Fray Junipero
Serra) and you will find bars,
discothèques and flamenco
venues all within a few steps of
each other. Some of the hotels
put on live music during the
season.

Restaurants
Lunchtimes are best spent on
Burriana beach where a good
selection of restaurants serve
mostly seafood menus. Huge
paellas are made daily
throughout the summer.
Restaurants within the town
cover a broad spectrum of
national and international
cuisines, including Chinese,
Indian, French and Italian.
Principal eating areas are in
and around Calle Almirante
Ferrándiz and Avenida Castilla
Perez.

Casa Luque, Plaza Cavana 2
(tel: 52 10 04). Varied selection
of national and international
dishes for all tastes, and at
moderate prices. The
homemade pâté, roast meats
and *crema catalana* (dessert)
are all recommended.

Pepe Rico, Calle Almirante
Ferrándiz 28 (tel: 52 02 47). Very
popular with all nationalities.
Top-class and imaginative
Swiss-French menu, presented
professionally and with a smile.
Prices are quite high but the
value is excellent. Book well in
advance.

Udo Heimer, Pueblo Andaluz 27
(tel: 52 00 32). Udo will probably
welcome you personally to his
attractively designed villa/
restaurant. Good choice of
interesting meat dishes, and
tasty seafood such as king
prawns wrapped in bacon with
a curry sauce. Leave room for
the delicious desserts.

Shopping

Principal shopping streets lie around the Balcón de Europa (stretching from Avenida Castilla Pérez to Calle Pintada), and include the modern shopping precinct of the same name that stands in front. The main local handicrafts are leather goods and ceramics. The weekly fleamarket attracts the most attention, with everything from pillow cases to antiques on display. It takes place in Calle Ruperto Andues and Calle Herrera Oria on Tuesday mornings.

Special Events

The celebrations of **San Isidro** (15 May) are popular and colourful, with many people wearing traditional dress. During July and August there are **festivals of music and dance** in the caves. These are highly recommended and should be booked in advance. Nerja's annual **fair** falls in the second week of October.

Sit back and brighten up for Nerja's Gran Fest de San Isidro

Sports

Watersports are offered on most of the beaches during the season, and some hotels have good tennis facilities. Do not be misled by references to the Nerja Golf urbanisation, since the course no longer exists.

◆
RINCÓN DE LA VICTORIA

Rincón de la Victoria has developed as a residential area and resort for the inhabitants of Málaga. Numerous apartment complexes and small pueblo-style urbanisations hug the shoreline, which offers long, though narrow, stretches of shallow sand beaches and dozens of beach restaurants. Most daytime activity takes place at the water's edge. Local amenities are fairly simple and attractions are limited.

The **Cueva del Higuerón** (known popularly as the Treasure Cave) supposedly guards the treasure of five Muslim kings who were fleeing Christian persecution. Its real fascination, however, lies in its great age. It was formed millions of years ago, sculpted under the sea by marine erosion. Palaeolithic paintings have been discovered in the lower chambers, and archaeological investigations prove it to have once been a neolithic necropolis (*Open:* 10.00–13.45 hrs and 16.00–18.45 hrs. *Closed:* Monday in winter.)

Accommodation

Rincón Sol, Avenida del Mediterráneo 24 (tel: 40 11 00), 3-star. The recently renovated hotel is now the most comfortable accommodation in the area, facing on to the beach.

Restaurants

The best place to eat is on the beach. A large number of restaurants, packed to bursting point during the summer, offer a variety of mainly fish menus. Local specialities include the *boquerones victorianos* (fresh anchovies), caught in the bay, and charcoal-cooked sardines.

Sports

Assorted watersports are available during the summer, and there is a new, 18-hole golf course at Benagalbón, called Añoreta Golf.

◆
TORRE DEL MAR

This is the beach suburb of the nearby municipal capital, Vélez-Málaga. Its coastal ribbon development of apartment blocks and urbanisations caters mostly to the summer requirements of Spanish tourists, attracted by the medium-priced facilities and huge beaches. Agriculture still plays an important role, however, and sugar cane fields, fruit orchards and market gardens – some still ploughed by oxen – continue to occupy land which could be sold at a high price for building. Tourist amenities are moderate by the standards of other resorts on the coast, but are developing fast.

First on the schedule for all children under 75 years old has to be a visit to **Aqua Velís**, an aquapark on the road to Vélez-Málaga. A karting track offers an alternative afternoon out for the kids, as does the **Fuerte El Dorado** (between Vélez-Málaga and Arenas) which puts on Wild West performances.

Accommodation

Most visitors either own their own apartments or rent them, and there is a shortage of hotel space. Simple accommodation for those passing through can be found at the 2-star hotels **Myrian** (tel: 54 13 00), and **Las Yucas** (tel: 54 22 72). Both have 72 rooms and are on the highway.

Restaurants

Local menus offer no special surprises, but prices are reasonable. Seafood is predictably the principal attraction along the seafront.

Sports

Watersports are popular during summer, and some sailing and windsurfing courses are available at the nautical club near the port.

◆
TORROX COSTA

Especially popular with German visitors, this long stretch of coastline has been fashioned into a dense amalgam of huge apartment complexes, Moorish-style urbanisations, numerous restaurants and more than a couple of *bierkellers*. The drab and styleless architecture of the 1970s is rapidly being replaced by imaginative, though equally large, modern developments all along the beach. Facilities of all sorts cater to the summer influx of tourists, though many close out of season.

The seemingly endless beach is the centre of most daytime activities, with watersports high on the list of demands. Bars, clubs and discothèques provide evening entertainment for most tastes. To the west lies Laguna Beach, a self-contained apartment complex providing most facilities for all ages in an attractive environment.

Accommodation

As with most of the eastern Costa del Sol, tourism is predominantly residential. The few hotels of the area are quite expensive for what they offer, and you would be best advised to rent an apartment for stays of more than a couple of days. For an overnight stop these small 2-star hotels are convenient: **Costa Mar** (tel: 53 00 49) and **Santa Rosa** (tel: 53 10 51), both on the main road and offering 49 and 22 rooms respectively.

Restaurants

A number of establishments serve predominantly German menus at predominantly German prices. Lunches are normally enjoyed in one of the many *chiringuitos*, or beach bars, which specialise in seafood and barbecues.

Sports

Summer activities are centred on the waterfront, with plenty of opportunities for windsurfing, waterskiing, jet-skiing, boat rental and so on. Most facilities close out of season.

LA AXARQUÍA – INLAND

Local authorities have designed five tourist routes with which to explore the Axarquía. These are colour-coded and signposted along the roads. Each itinerary loosely follows a theme: the **Sun and Avocado Route** follows the rich flatlands of the river Vélez valley; the **Sun and Wine Route** takes in the principal wine-producing villages, including Frigiliana and Competa; the **Mudéjar Route** centres on small villages of the Sierra de Almijara, with some interesting Mudéjar architecture; the **Raisin Route** lies to the west of the river Vélez among the lower hillsides; and the **Oil and Mountain Route** passes through the higher villages and olive-growing areas in the northern Axarquía. Tourist offices will supply you with full details plus a map.

WHAT TO SEE

◆
ALCAUCÍN

Bordering the lower slopes of the Sierra de Tejeda and the natural park of El Alcázar,

Alcaucín was first occupied during Phoenician times. The Moors refortified the village which, after the Christian Reconquest, took part in the Rebellion of the Alpujarras. A local drama, the murder of an innkeeper and his family, sparked off a wave of tortures and executions of the local Moors, and helped precipitate fierce support for the rebellion. Natural features of the area include the beautiful mountain pass of Zafarraya leading into Granada province; the Alcázar park, whose entrance lies only three miles (4.5km) from the village; and the natural sulphur springs of Las Majadas. Excellent views can be had from the 18th-century hermitage near the graveyard. The best times to visit are for the pilgrimage of San Isidro on 15 May, which takes place in the park, the summer fiestas of San Agustín in the second week of August or the bonfires of La Candelaria on 8 September.

◆
ALGARROBO
Although it is the administrative centre for the heavily urbanised beach area known as Algarrobo Costa, the village economy remains firmly rooted in farming. Tomatoes, avocados, strawberries and water melons are the principal products. The liveliest fiestas are San Sebastián in January, with a procession and fireworks, and the August fair.

◆
ALMÁCHAR
Situated in the heartland of 'raisin country', Almáchar has

numerous constructions that look rather like burial plots in a giant's graveyard. These are *paseros*, or drying frames for the grapes, and can be seen throughout most of the Axarquía, though not usually in such numbers.

The village's claim to fame is its almond and garlic soup, which becomes the centre of celebrations during the Fiesta de Ajoblanco in August. Other events include a pilgrimage (on the first Sunday of May) which dates from the 18th century, and the summer fair at the end of July.

◆◆
ARCHEZ
Tiny, and largely ignored by the passing world, Archez is worth visiting just for a look at its delightful minaret, now declared a historic monument. Built in the 14th century, it is a perfect example of the imaginative geometry and simple elegance of Nasrid architecture (the same style as the Alhambra in Granada). Today a church has replaced the former mosque and the tower is capped by a small but complementary belfry.

◆
ARENAS
After a steep climb out of Vélez-Málaga into the Sierra de Almijara, Arenas is the starting point of the Mudéjar Route. Large alluvial deposits of sand (*arena*), now used for gritting the snowbound mountain passes, gave the village its name. King Ferdinand stayed here during the conquest of Vélez-Málaga, and its strategic importance is demonstrated by the nearby remains of Bentomiz

castle – a Moorish construction on Roman foundations of which only the cellars and a few walls survive. From the castle you can enjoy sweeping views of the coast and valley. One and a half miles (2.5km) further up the road lies an interesting 16th-century Mudéjar style church and adjacent Moorish fountain.

Drinking fountain, Competa

◆
BENAMOCARRA
The old part of Benamocarra still preserves the atmosphere and much of the architecture of the original Moorish town, although in 1572 it was entirely resettled by Christians from Antequera and Seville. The composer and musician Eduardo Ocón was born here in 1833. Fiestas include the pilgrimage during San Isidro (15 May) and the celebrations for the village's patron saint during the last week of October.

◆
EL BORGE
Curiously set astride a small river gorge, the village is known locally as the capital of the moscatel grape, because of the importance of its grape harvest. Its rebellious and independent spirit has been demonstrated on two occasions, first by its fierce support of the Moorish uprising, and then later by one of its inhabitants – 'El Bizco de Borge' – who became Málaga's most feared bandit during the late 19th century. For once the local church is well worth a visit, being a curious Mudéjar interpretation of Gothic and Renaissance styles, built in the early 16th century.

◆◆◆
COMPETA
During the last few years Competa has become a popular home for foreign writers, artists and those wishing to escape the 20th-century bustle along the coast. The old town, perched on a long mountain spur, is a pleasant mixture of old and modern architecture in keeping with its mountain location. Surrounding farmsteads show clear evidence of the area's new-found wealth, and many have been converted into the semi-luxurious holiday homes of both foreigners and Spaniards. Local agriculture is based on the grape in all its forms, and the town's bodegas produce a range of justifiably popular wines. These are best enjoyed (for free) during the Noche del Vino (Night of Wine) on 15 August, along with music and dance.

You should stop before entering Competa to enjoy the superb views of the town, clustered around its prominent baroque church. If you want to spend the night, there is a simple but acceptable *hostal* in the main square, where you will also find a reasonable selection of small eating houses and bars.

◆◆◆
FRIGILIANA

This white village has become the most popular excursion destination from Nerja. It lies about four miles (6km) inland, draped over the lower slopes of the Sierra de Tejeda and surrounded by terraced vegetable gardens and fruit orchards. Narrow, twisting streets wander up the hill between dazzlingly whitewashed houses to the top of the town, where there are spectacular views of the coastline and rolling foothills. You might expect such a strategic vantage point to have a castle, and indeed there used to be one. Though both Phoenician and Roman remains have been found in the area, it was the Moors who constructed a seemingly impregnable fortress. During the rebellion of the Alpujarras (1568), Frigiliana became the final stronghold of the rebels until they were overwhelmed by hugely outnumbering Christian forces. The castle was completely destroyed and the surviving villagers were deported. Ceramic plaques in some of the streets vividly commemorate the dramatic siege.

There are a number of interesting craft shops and galleries in the back streets of the old village, but perhaps the most popular 'souvenir' of the area is the tasty local wine. During Holy Week the locals stage a passion play in the church, with actors dressed in 18th-century costume. In June the Christian victory over the Moors is commemorated with colourful processions, music and cultural events.

◆
MACHARAVIAYA

This tiny, unassuming village has had a surprisingly illustrious past. It was very prosperous during the 18th and early 19th centuries, thanks partly to its successful grape cultivation and partly to the manufacture of playing cards, which were

High-rise development in Frigiliana

exported to Spain's colonies in South America. The area's fortunes were sponsored largely by the Gálvez family, who also attracted the cream of the intelligentsia. Poets and painters spent summers in the area, which soon became labelled 'little Madrid'. In 1857 the popular modernist poet Salvador Rueda was born here. Today, Macharaviaya is receiving attention once again as a natural extension to the coastal development, with villas and small urbanisations dotting the landscape. The baroque church is worth a glance for its marble work and a handful of 17th-century paintings. The entire crypt is dedicated to the Gálvez family.

◆
MOCLINEJO
Scene of an overwhelming defeat of Christian forces by the Moors in 1482, the village still preserves its memories in street names such as 'Hoya de los Muertos' (Vale of the Dead) and 'Cuesta de la Matanza' (Massacre Hill). The otherwise undistinguished church, reconstructed in the 18th century, has interesting modernist ironwork in the choir.

◆
PERIANA
Steep, rocky hillsides surround the town and its olive and fruit orchards. Unlike most of the Axarquian villages, Periana is relatively modern and was first given its municipal independence in the late 18th century. The peaches grown here are considered by many to be the finest in Spain, and in

early September the Fiesta de Melocotón (Peach Fiesta) animates the whole town with tastings, auctions and cultural events. Near by, at the natural spa of Baños de Vilo, you can see the remains of Moorish baths which were still in use during the 19th century.

◆◆
SALARES
This is one of the stops on the Mudéjar Route, and lies in a surprisingly green landscape. Local vineyards grow the Rome variety of grape (rather than the moscatel which is more usual in the area), and it produces an exceptionally rich wine. This is best sampled during the local fiestas of San Antón (17 January) and Santa Ana (26 July). Both olives and grapes are pressed in the village, following traditional methods.
The village's main 'sight' is its charming 13th-century Moorish minaret, now adjoining the church. It has been declared a historic monument, along with the minaret of Archez, and is of the same style.

◆
SEDELLA
Abundant springs and small watercourses irrigate numerous vegetable gardens in the immediate vicinity of Sedella, while traditional dry land orchards of vine, olive and almond climb the steeper slopes. Local tradition has an explanation of how the village received its name: Queen Isabel, upon being informed of a nearby victory by the Catholic forces, replied *'Sé de ella'* ('I know about it'). The village was

later given to Diego Fernández de Córdoba in recognition of his support during the Christian Reconquest, and his house, with its curious Mudéjar tower, lies near the church.

◆◆
TORROX

Although Torrox is only a couple of miles (4km) from its beach suburb Torrox Costa, the two are worlds apart in atmosphere. While Torrox Costa is a modern resort, the older community still has the tranquillity of a relaxed and rural community.

Judging by the discovery of villas, a necropolis and thermal baths, the Romans established an important community in the area, although it was mainly on the coast. Mosaics and utensils from the period are now housed in museums in Málaga and Barcelona. Under Moorish rule, Torrox became the centre of valuable silk and sugar industries, and is claimed to be the birthplace of the great Moorish vizier, Almanzor, in AD938.

A wander around the back streets will lead you to the 16th-century Franciscan convent, constructed in the Mudéjar style and now being converted into a hotel. Near by is the old 19th-century sugar factory and an 18th-century building that used to be a mint (Casa de la Moneda).

Among other annual events, the Fiesta de las Migas is held on the Sunday before Christmas, with *migas* (a fried snack) and the local country wines served everywhere, along with cultural events, music and dancing.

◆◆
VÉLEZ-MÁLAGA

Capital of the Axarquía, Vélez has the third largest population in the province. Tourism predominates in its beach suburb, Torre del Mar, while most trade and processing of the local products takes place in the commercial districts around the city's outskirts. For visitors it offers the interest of the daily workings of a Spanish town, and a handful of unpretentious monuments. Here you can still enjoy 'discovering' a town that lies well off the beaten tourist track, in spite of its proximity to the coast.

Phoenicians, Greeks and Romans were all aware of the strategic location and founded settlements in the vicinity. It was the Moors who laid out much of the town as you see it today and developed its industries. During the 14th and 15th centuries, it became a key defensive post of the kingdom of Granada, as well as an important commercial and cultural centre. In 1487 the town surrendered to the forces of Ferdinand and, without a capital, most of the Axarquía quickly followed suit.

Today, huge *corridas* (warehouses) act as clearing points for the region's fruit, vegetables, oils and other products. There is some light industry in furniture, decorative metal products and ceramics, while smaller workshops concentrate on local crafts such as small scale pottery production, saddle-making and canework. Near the coast lies an important sugar factory. Above the town stand the

remains of its 13th-century Moorish **castle**, largely destroyed during the War of the Spanish Succession (1704) and recently restored. It gives fine views of the area. To one side lies the oldest quarter of town, known as **Arrabal de San Sebastián**, which dates from the 15th century. Here you can take a wander through haphazardly planned back streets that have changed little in 500 years. Below the castle are further medieval districts, where some of the houses exhibit curious architectural details from the north of Spain, such as large overhanging eaves. These were clearly inspired by Asturian immigrants, who repopulated the town in the 16th century. Of the numerous churches and convents, only **Santa María la Mayor** warrants attention. Started immediately after the town's conquest (1487) on the site of the old mosque, it is in the Mudéjar style.

Accommodation

There is little in town except for a couple of small hotels aimed at the commercial traveller. Most people look for accommodation along the coast.

In the heart of rich agricultural land, Vélez-Málaga is still dominated by its Moorish castle

Restaurants

Most facilities lie out of town, in the beach urbanisations, though you will come across plenty of small bars and restaurants serving local menus at reasonable prices.

Special Events

The **Fiestas de Mayo** cover a week at the end of April and beginning of May in celebration of the Christian Reconquest, with street parties, sports and cultural events. The processions during Holy Week are the biggest in the Axarquía.

◆
VIÑUELA

Set astride a once-busy highway, Viñuela is a relatively modern cluster of houses around a 16th-century church and delightful *venta* (inn). The latter has changed little since it was built more than 200 years ago and is well worth a visit to sample the local wine and have a snack. Local farming has taken on a new lease of life since the construction of the nearby reservoir.

TORREMOLINOS

The coast to the west of Málaga has been intensively developed for tourism, and has the most famous resorts of the Costa del Sol. The first west of Málaga is Torremolinos, perhaps the most famous of all.

It is hard to believe that only 40 years ago Torremolinos was a tiny coastal village with one main street and only a score of houses. Since the advent of organised tourism to the coast, unprecedented expansion has converted this small fishing community into Spain's ultimate package holiday destination, and a household name in a dozen countries.

Torremolinos derives its name from the old watchtower that still stands sentinel above Bajondillo beach, and which once protected the numerous water-fed flour mills (*torre* means tower, *molinos* means mills). In 1930 the natural springs were diverted to feed nearby Málaga, and without water the mills soon fell into disuse.

The excellent climate, nearby airport and superb beaches made Torremolinos the perfect site for mass tourism. Uninhibited low-cost development during the 1960s created a concrete jungle that was designed to fulfil every tourist requirement, at a price that anyone could afford. The local environment suffered from such careless commercialism, and today many parts of the town desperately need a facelift.

Torremolinos remains a holiday paradise, however. Countless hotels, apartments, bars, pubs, restaurants, discothèques, boutiques and souvenir shops offer everything that a family on vacation might need or want, especially if they are young and active. Daytime activities centre on the large sand beaches with their numerous watersports, while the resort's nightlife is the busiest along the Costa del Sol. Torremolinos is split into three principal areas. The town centre contains the major shopping zones, restaurants and evening bars. El Bajondillo and Playamar, to the east along the seafront, accommodate most of the big hotels and watersports facilities. La Carihuela and Montemar, to the west, offer more large beachfront hotels, fish restaurants and a wide choice of nightlife.

WHAT TO SEE

◆◆◆
ATLANTIS AQUAPARK
Carretera Nacional 340 (near congress centre)
Fun and excitement for all ages – and an excellent opportunity to forget about the kids, who will be carefully watched by the numerous lifeguards and monitors. Attractions include waterslides, wave pools and a special mini-park for children. There are also cafeterias, bars and gift shops.
Open: 10.00–21.00 hrs from April until October.

◆◆
CUESTA DEL TAJO
This steep winding walkway starts beside the 14th-century Moorish watchtower at the end

of Calle San Miguel, and leads down through the old fishermen's quarter to El Bajondillo and the beach. Now lined with souvenir shops, bars and restaurants, it is all that remains of the original village. Watch out for the attractive 16th-century **Molino La Bóveda**, once a flour mill and now converted into a restaurant and flamenco venue.

Accommodation

Torremolinos has approximately 100 different hotels and 4,000 apartments. You can find 5-star accommodation if you want it, though most visitors stay at one of the 3- or 4-star hotels, which offer reliable facilities at reasonable prices. Apartment rental, with or without hotel services, is increasingly popular and may be the most economical holiday base for family groups. Budget lodgings are best looked for around the Plaza Costa del Sol in the centre, and just off Carihuela beach.

Town Centre

Cervantes, Calle La Mercedes (tel: 38 40 33), 4-star. Spacious, modern and highly popular hotel in the heart of town. Covered rooftop pool and restaurant with excellent views. 400 rooms.
Castillo de Santa Clara, Calle Suecia 1 (tel: 38 31 55). Hotel apartment complex offering a wealth of facilities for all the family. It stands perched on the rocky bluff that separates the town's principal beaches, a short walk from the city centre. Guests can choose

from either regular hotel accommodation or apartments.

Montemar and La Carihuela

A number of small pensions line the back streets and beachfront of La Carihuela, offering simple facilities at realistic prices in a busy location. For more upmarket accommodation around here, try:
Meliá Torremolinos, Avenida Carlota Alessandri 104 (tel: 38 05 00), 5-star. Spacious and stylish hotel of 284 rooms, lying between the main road and beach. Mature tropical gardens border a pleasant pool area. Bedrooms are large and very tastefully decorated; the majority of them have sea and garden views. Luxury suites also available.
Aloha Puerto Sol, Vía Imperial

Apartment complex, Torremolinos

55 (tel: 38 70 86), 4-star. Huge hotel with three pools, 420 rooms and most amenities. Right on the beach.

Pez Espada, Vía Imperial 11 (tel: 38 03 00), 4-star. Well located on the best beach in town. Summer prices are rather high, but it becomes very good value out of season.

Tropicana, Calle Trópico 6 (tel: 38 66 00), 4-star. Intimately styled and colourful hotel on Carihuela beach, with cabana-style restaurant and beach club.

Lago Rojo, Calle Miami 1 (tel: 38 76 66), 3-star. In the centre of Carihuela, and only a short walk from the beach. The 144 rooms are attractively designed split-level studios.

Miami, Calle Aladino 14 (tel: 38 52 55), 2-star. Delightful villa-style hotel in the Andalucian style. Decorated by Manuel Blasco Alarcón, Picasso's cousin, it has an interesting and arty feel. Its 26 rooms offer facilities in keeping with its category.

El Bajondillo and Playamar

Don Pablo, Paseo Marítimo (tel: 38 38 88), 4-star. Beachfront hotel with 443 rooms which include 11 suites, 16 semi-suites

and 134 'executive' rooms (with satellite TV). A large banquet hall, stylish discothèque, full conference facilities and a tennis club make this a comprehensive hotel.

Meliá Costa del Sol, Paseo Marítimo (tel: 38 66 77), 4-star. Huge but handsome hotel with 540 rooms, comprising singles, doubles, suites and semi-suites. It is perfectly located for beach and town with a wealth of entertainment and sports facilities, except, surprisingly, for tennis.

Principe Sol, Paseo del Colorado 26 (tel: 38 41 00), 3-star. The largest establishment in town, with 600 rooms (some are apartments), located right on the beach and with most facilities for the tourist.

Out of Town

Parador de Golf (tel: 38 12 55), 4-star. A secluded and peaceful national parador beside the golf course. It lies near the airport, right on the beach, about two and a half miles (4km) from Torremolinos. This is an excellent place to get away

La Carihuela beach, Torremolinos: sun, sea, sky and swimming

from it all and enjoy the comprehensive sports facilities. 40 rooms.

Nightlife

Whatever you may think of the evening's opportunities in Torremolinos, you need never be bored. Discothèques, clubs, pubs, music bars, flamenco, live shows of all descriptions and an endless series of summer parties animate the whole town until it shakes. The Plaza Costa del Sol is especially vibrant, and is packed with a young crowd even out of season.

There are more than 80 discothèques to choose from, of which the **Palladium**, Avenida Palma de Mallorca 36, is the most impressive, with its four dance floors, five bars, swimming pool and pizzeria. More discothèques line the Plaza Costa del Sol, Avenida Carlota Alessandri (where you will find **Number One**, actually at number 10), and Avenida Montemar, where there are **Gatsby** and **Joy**. Most establishments mount fiestas, competitions and theme parties throughout the summer. Flamenco is highly popular and there are many tablaos to choose from. **Pepe Lopez**, Plaza Gamba Alegre, and **Pepe Marchena**, Avenida Carlota Alessandri 135, are among the best known. Occasional shows and live music can be found at **Molino de la Bóveda**, an old water mill in the Cuesta del Tajo. Most hotels put on nightly shows throughout the season, including cabaret, flamenco, popular dancing and competitions.

Restaurants

Finding a restaurant in Torremolinos is no problem – it is deciding which to choose that takes the time. Fish dishes are the main attraction along the beachfront, particularly in La Carihuela where almost every house serves seafood in one form or another, and many exhibit tempting displays of the daily catch. The most common dish on their menus is the *fritura malagueña*, or mixed fried fish. Most international menus are similar, as are the prices, which are aimed at the tourist on a budget. Foreign cuisine is well represented, and you can choose from British, French, Italian, German, Scandinavian, Chinese, Vietnamese and others. There is also a vegetarian restaurant and some restaurants serve Spanish regional food, including Galician, Basque, Castilian and Catalan.

Fast food comes in every shape, size, colour and flavour, from burgers to ice cream to German sausages. You need never go short of an English breakfast or a handful of fish and chips. Some stalls sell seafood by weight.

City Centre

The large pedestrian precincts of La Nogalera and Pueblo Blanco, on either side of Calle Casablanca, contain dozens of eateries. **Las Pampas**, Calle Guetaria (tel: 38 65 59) is an Argentine grill serving meat platters at moderate prices. Close by in Pueblo Blanco, more intimate surroundings are found in **El Atrio** (tel: 38 88 50) along

Beached on the Costa del Sol

with an imaginative French menu. Almost next door, the **León de Castilla** (tel: 38 69 59) offers a more conventional selection of international dishes. In the same urbanisation you will find a small vegetarian snack bar. The **Florida**, Calle Casablanca 15 (tel: 38 50 95) is medium-priced and allows a free choice of food from its open buffet. Fresh seafood is sold by weight at **La Chacha** in the Plaza Costa del Sol.

Montemar and La Carihuela
Wander La Carihuela seafront and choose at will from the endless selection of fish and seafood restaurants. Old favourites are **Casa Prudencio, El Roqueo** and **Moncho**. Cheaper and simpler is **Casa Juan**, lying one street back. The **Pizza All' Incontro**, Bloque Euromar, Avenida Montemar

101, serves tasty Italian dishes cooked in a wood-fire oven. The nearby **Normandie**, Centro Comercial Montemar (tel: 38 43 58) is best for French cuisine, at a price.

El Bajondillo and Playamar
You will find mostly snack food and conventional mixed dishes along the seafront, and fish served in the beach bars. It is best to visit the town centre if you want a wider selection.

Shopping
The whole town is a jumbled mass of boutiques, souvenir shops and clothing stores. Fierce competition has kept prices to a minimum and you can find some good bargains, particularly in leather goods. Principal shopping areas are along Calle San Miguel and

among the labyrinthine passages and arcades leading off to either side. The municipal market is near the bypass, in Calle Periodista Antonio Sáenz, also site of the Thursday fleamarket.

Special Events
The **Fiestas de San Miguel** are held for a week around 29 September, with a large fair in Avenida Imperial, competitions and live entertainment. On the Sunday there is a colourful procession to Pinares los Manantiales.

Sports
Bowling alley Bowling Montemar, Avenida Montemar 68.
Bowls Costa del Sol Bowls Club, Torremolinos Beach Club, Playa El Lido.
Golf Club de Campo de Málaga, next to the Parador (tel: 38 12 55). Oldest course on the coast, 18 holes.
Horseriding El Ranchito, La Colina, Camino del Pilar (tel: 38 30 63) rental and tuition; Hípica Internacional, Churriana (tel: 43 55 49), classes only.
Mini golf Aquagolf, next to the aquapark, open all year. One of the largest in the country, 18 holes.
Tennis Hotel Don Pablo, Paseo Marítimo, Bajondillo; Club de Tenis Torremolinos, Las Viñas, Churriana (tel: 43 51 25). Many of the hotels, such as Pez Espada and Aloha Puerto Sol, have courts for hire.
Watersports Summer facilities are plentiful along the beaches, with a big choice of equipment rental and tuition, particularly in front of the big hotels.

BENALMÁDENA COSTA

This section covers Benalmádena Costa, its inland parent village Benalmádena Pueblo, and the rapidly expanding Arroyo de la Miel that lies between the two. Limited space and rapid development have blurred the distinction between the areas, though all three have distinct characters and attractions. The background setting is pretty, with mountain slopes rising swiftly towards the Sierra de Mijas. Every inch of the short coastline, still dangerously squeezed by the fast main road, has been developed, with numerous hotels and restaurants bordering the seafront promenade and narrow sand beaches. On the eastern boundary with Torremolinos is a large sports-port and stylish residential complex, very much the flagship of the area and still being developed. At the opposite end of the beachfront lies the Torrequebrada urbanisation, with golf course, casino and nightclub. Benalmádena Pueblo lies about five miles (8km) from the sea amid a rocky hillside dotted with villas. Though heavily developed it still preserves its intimate small-town atmosphere, with narrow whitewashed streets and a pretty central square. Founded by the Moors (probably on the site of a Roman settlement), it is now the focus of a predominantly residential community, operating at half the pace of anything on the coast. Arroyo de la Miel is almost entirely modern and has developed from a few farmhouses and villas into a suburban sprawl that is the service centre of the municipality. Near by is the Tivoli World amusement park. Here, as on the coast, English is the predominant foreign language and there is a large range of sports, and other facilities for tourists.

WHAT TO SEE

◆◆◆
BENALMÁDENA PUEBLO

The village is an award-winner for being the prettiest in the province, and provides a welcome break from the coast. Its small church and surrounding gardens afford panoramic views of the countryside. Narrow back streets house a handful of craft shops, restaurants, and the interesting archaeological museum (separate entry).

◆
CASTILLO BIL-BIL

Carretera Nacional 340, Benalmádena Costa
This is an exhibition centre in mock-Moorish surroundings. Various art shows and occasional live music are put on, and it makes a venue for theatre, music and dance during the summer festivals. Check the local press or tourist office for details.
Open: (winter) 10.00–14.00 hrs and 18.00–21.00 hrs; (summer) 17.00–23.00 hrs.

◆◆◆
MUSEO ARQUEOLÓGICO

Avenida Juan Peralta, Benalmádena Pueblo

The compact but fascinating collection comes mainly from Nicaragua and Peru, before Columbus' discovery of the New World. There are also some local finds from the neolithic, Iberian and Roman eras. The museum acts as a tourist office.
Open: (weekdays) 10.00–14.00 hrs and 16.00–19.00 hrs; (Saturday and Sunday) 10.00–14.00 hrs. Closed Monday.

◆◆◆
PUERTO MARINA

Benalmádena Costa
This huge sports-port, with anchorage for almost 1,000 boats, contains an equally large and inspired residential development, almost a village on its own. Design is modern and very stylish, the facilities are varied and are growing every day. On Sundays and during the season, its restaurants and bars are packed – this is *the* place to be.

◆◆◆
TIVOLI WORLD

Arroyo de la Miel
The 25 acres (10 hectares) of fairground and gardens contain attractions for all the family. The entrance fee includes more than 30 rides, and there are restaurants, bars and shops. Live shows take place nightly, and frequently feature 'big name' performers. Tourist offices will have current details. *Open:* 17.00 hrs until late. Closed November to March.

Accommodation
Almost all the hotels are to be found along the coast, on either side of the national highway, and many are 3-star with similar

Benalmádena: Castillo Bil Bil

outlooks and facilities. A couple of pensions offer cheaper lodgings in Arroyo de la Miel. **Torrequebrada**, Carretera Nacional 340 (tel: 44 60 00), 5-star. Top class services and excellent sports facilities are complemented by a 5-fork restaurant, plus a casino, nightclub and health centre. The large and protected beach is busy in the summer. The 284 rooms include over 60 suites, and prices are high.
Riviera, Avenida Antonio Machado 49 (tel: 44 12 40), 4-star. Convenient for shops and the port, with split-level garden areas leading to the beach. The 189 rooms have good views.
Sunset Beach Club, Carretera Nacional 340 (tel: 44 58 40). Very modern and comfortable complex with 400 single-bedroom apartments. Full sports, entertainments and other services that compare with 4-star hotel standards.
La Roca, Carretera Nacional 340 (tel: 44 17 40), 3-star. Old-fashioned but friendly, with large gardens and adequate facilities. 157 rooms.

Los Patos, Carretera Nacional 340 (tel: 44 19 90), 3-star. Smartly run and comfortable hotel that deserves a better rating. Enormous pool and extensive tropical gardens. 270 rooms.
Mozart, Calle La Malagueña s/n (tel: 44 19 99), 3-star. Small establishment in residential area that is quiet and relatively secluded. 43 rooms.

Nightlife
For a full choice of bars, discothèques and flamenco shows you are advised to visit Torremolinos. The Montemar area of Torremolinos is within walking distance of the sports-port. Otherwise most activity is confined to Plaza Solymar, opposite the port entrance, where a young crowd packs the handful of bars and discothèques, such as **Borsalino Palace** and **Plus**. Another busy dance floor is that of **Rich**, Edificio Maite 1, towards the other end of the seafront. Flamenco can be found around Arroyo de la Miel at **El Tano**,

BENALMÁDENA COSTA

Carretera Nacional 340, and **El Patio de Anales**, Avenida García Lorca. While in the port, you should check out **Puerto Rociero**.

The **Fortuna** nightclub (tel: 38 31 40) and **Casino Torrequebrada** (tel: 44 25 45), Carretera Nacional 340, are in the Torrequebrada urbanisation at the western end of the shoreline. Both offer a sophisticated welcome to those who are looking for either a high-class floorshow or a spell at the gaming tables, and the Fortuna hosts renowned classical ballet performances as well. The nightclub opens at 21.30 hrs except Sundays and the casino times are 20.00–04.00 hrs. Also here are a discothèque, restaurant, piano bar and cafeteria.

Big concerts and floorshows are often staged in Tivoli World, and there may be a play or concert on at the Casa de Cultura in Arroyo de la Miel.

Restaurants

There are few outstanding restaurants among the hundreds of eating establishments, which mostly lie on the coast and in Arroyo de la Miel. Fast food and tourist menus proliferate. A few places are worth looking out for, however:

Arroyo de la Miel

Both the **Mesón del Virrey**, Avenida de la Constitución 87 (tel: 44 35 99) and the adjacent **Ventorrillo de la Perra** (tel: 44 19 66) are worth sampling for their creative Malagan cooking, particularly the meats. Both occupy old buildings, and have summer terraces and rustic atmospheres. The former is closed on Wednesday and the latter on Monday.

Benalmádena Costa

Try **Senang**, Plaza Flamingo 1 (tel: 44 48 31) for Indonesian cooking. A general favourite is the 20-dish rice table, though the prices are high. Closed Monday. Not far away is **Chef Alonso**, Carretera Nacional 340 (tel: 44 34 35), with a solid reputation for its menu and fast service.

Mamma Mía, also on the main road, provides the old Italian favourites at economical prices. In the marina there are further choices of Chinese, Italian and French restaurants.

Benalmádena Pueblo

La Rueda, Calle San Miguel 2 (tel: 44 82 21) is attractively priced and popular enough to warrant a trip from the coast. The international menu is recommended for its lamb and chicken dishes. Closed Tuesday.

Shopping

Most shops are in Arroyo de la Miel and on the coast, offering the standard range of holiday goods, clothes and souvenirs. For a wider selection and better prices, you would do best to visit Torremolinos or Málaga. A number of fashionable boutiques in the port offer quality goods at higher prices. Weekly fleamarkets are held on Fridays in Benalmádena, Calle Felipe Orlando, and outside Tivoli World, Arroyo de la Miel. A supermarket offers 24-hour service in the Edificio Alay near the port entrance.

Special Events

Holy Week in Benalmádena is well known for its processions and enactment of 'El Paso' on a large open-air stage, often drawing crowds of up to 15,000 people. **Corpus Christi** (May/June) sees other religious processions, this time over petal-strewn streets. **San Juan** is celebrated on 24 June in Arroyo de la Miel, with a week of festivities culminating in the ritual burning of dolls on the evening before the saint's day. The coast has to wait until 16 July before it can welcome its own **Veladilla del Carmen** fiestas. These incorporate sea processions. In the middle of the following month, on 15 August, the **Virgen de la Cruz** is yet another good reason to participate in the fun. Throughout both July and August there are a multitude of other happenings, including theatre, music and dance, many of which take place in the **Casa de Cultura**, Plaza Asturia, Arroyo de la Miel (tel: 44 46 89). Check here too for other events throughout the year.

Sports

Golf Golf Torrequebrada, Carretera Nacional 340 (tel: 44 27 42). 18-hole course, squash courts and sauna.

Spectator sports Most occur in Arroyo de la Miel. At the Polideportivo you can watch or participate in a variety of field sports such as football, cricket and hockey. There are tennis courts and a running track; El Tomillar is an artificial grass stadium. A new sports centre is being built in Benalmádena.

Squash Hotels Torrequebrada and San Fermín (tel: 44 20 40).

Tennis Some hotels, including Torrequebrada, Tritón (tel: 44 32 40) and Riviera, have courts. The Riviera's is artificial grass.

Watersports There are board sports on the beaches during summer. Arroyo de la Miel and Benalmádena have municipal swimming pools. The Club Náutico (tel: 44 22 45) in the port is one of the most active along the coast for hosting regattas and other events.

Echoes of Moorish minarets at Benalmádena Costa's yacht marina

FUENGIROLA AND MIJAS

Fuengirola's young mariners

FUENGIROLA AND MIJAS

As with other places along the coast, there is a romantic tradition that Fuengirola was once a pretty fishing village where people lived an undisturbed life, and that all that has been ruined by tourist development. It is truer to say that before the tourist boom there was a poor and tatty village on an unwanted coast, where people eked out a miserable life. It is people with money in their pockets, usually foreigners and writers, who wistfully recall a scene and life they did not endure. You would be hard pressed to find a local person who wanted a return to the bad old days. It is much the same in Mijas, the transformed hillside village from which Fuengirola gained independence in 1841. The town's main activity of the past is commemorated by the Monumento al Pescador (fisherman) on the Paseo Marítimo.

Otherwise there is not much evidence of local history, though there was a settlement known as Suel by the Romans and as Sohail by the Moors. You can take your pick from two explanations for the present name: the village gained the nickname of 'Girona' during the 18th century, when the area was engaged in Genoa's maritime trade, and from that Fuengirola was derived; or it was named 'Font-jirola' after a fountain at the foot of the castle. Sohail Castle, on the western edge of town, was first built by the Moors in AD956 and was destroyed after the Christian conquest of the area in 1485. The present structure was built in 1730 and is being converted into a cultural centre. It is a good spot from which to get a view over the town and the coast.

Most of Fuengirola's long beachfront of over four miles (7km) is backed by a promenade and line of high-rise blocks. There is hardly a plot left for building in its municipal area. In the large area run by Mijas, which reaches the sea along the seven-and-a-half-mile (12km) stretch of Mijas-Costa, foreigners resident in many spreading urbanisations already outnumber the municipality's Spanish residents. It is not difficult to foresee the growth of an extended urban mass stretching from sea to mountain with clumps of green spaces, mostly provided by golf courses. Mijas already has eight and more are planned. Package tourism predominates in Fuengirola, which appeals mainly to young families and older people, the latter arriving throughout the year. It is more sedate than Torremolinos, less self-conscious and costly than Marbella. Residential tourism is more usual within the area of Mijas, but a lot of short-stay, self-catering apartment accommodation is rising along its share of the coast.

The large urbanisation of Torreblanca del Sol, facing Playas de Carvajal and Gaviotas on the other side of the N340 highway, lies on Fuengirola's eastern boundary. Next comes Playa de los Boliches, backed by the part of town with the same name, derived from *bolicheros* (shopkeepers). Beyond the Puerto Deportivo (Sports-Port) is Playa de Santa Amalia. Beaches are mostly of fine or coarse dark sand and are well serviced, except during winter, with many amenities and sports. Across the Río de Fuengirola and up to Faro de Calaburras (lighthouse) is Playa de la Campaña. Further west, Playa de la Cala de Mijas and other beaches with rocky outcrops lie close to the N340 highway and serve a fast-growing crop of urbanisations along Mijas's coast, such as Miraflores and Torrenueva. Long-established and virtually self-contained Calahonda abuts with Marbella's boundary. Inland, more urbanisations like Mijas Golf, and hotel complexes, like the luxurious Byblos Andaluz, are overlooked by the village which clings to its mountain.

WHAT TO SEE

FUENGIROLA
As with the other coastal towns, there is not much in the way of memorable sights in Fuengirola, but it has some pleasant places to pass the time. The **Plaza de la Constitución** is dominated by the main church, and surrounding bars have seating outdoors. Some nearby streets retain vestiges of their past. A few, like Calles Cruz and Moncayo, have been pedestrianised and it is pleasant to have a meal at outdoor tables and watch the passers by. A replica Roman façade in the **Plaza de Castilla** in Los Boliches is built of marble blocks which date from Roman times and were found locally. Animal lovers will probably want to avoid the **zoo** until conditions for the animals are improved. The **Parque Acuático Mijas**, on the town side of the N340 highway, is open from May to the end of September, with slides, pools and other amenities as an alternative to the beach. Andalucian artists have done large murals on some buildings which have brightened up the town and made a walk around it more interesting. Art showings and other events are held in the modern **Casa de Cultura** and in certain hotels and a few other venues.

MIJAS
Some 1,400 feet (425m) up from sea level, Mijas has back streets where you can catch the ambience of a modernised, peaceful pueblo, especially

after the tour coaches have left in the late afternoon. You can take rides around the village in a horsedrawn carriage or on the back of a *burro taxi* (donkey taxi). These can also be taken up to the small **Ermita del Puerto** chapel on the mountainside above the town. Near the main car, coach and donkey park is the cavelike **shrine of La Virgen de la Peña**, patron of Mijas. A **mobile museum** has an odd collection of minute and unusual things which is fun to see. There is an unusually square and tiny **bullring** but it is relatively costly to view and see its small collection of bull memorabilia. Near by is a church with Mudéjar elements. In front of it, the *mirador* affords extensive views across Mijas Campo to the coast and Fuengirola. In the old town hall, a **museum of popular arts** has tools, photographs and the like from the village's past. The small open-air auditorium hosts events during the summer.

Accommodation
Along Avenida de los Boliches are four low-cost places at which you can look for a simple room: **Santa Fe**, at number 66 (tel: 47 41 81); **El Amigo**, 71 (tel: 47 03 33); **Sarasol**, 87 (tel: 47 03 44); and **Costabella**, 114 (tel: 47 46 31).
This is a small selection of more upmarket hotels from the many available:
Byblos Andaluz, Mijas Golf (tel: 47 30 50, fax: 47 67 83), 5-star Gran Lujo, 135 rooms. Set in beautiful gardens, this is one of Spain's top hotels, with prices to match. Among its excellent leisure and sports amenities, the Louison Bobet Talasoterapia Instituto offers health and relaxation therapy.
Mijas, Urbanización Tamisa, Mijas (tel: 48 58 00, fax: 48 58 25), 4-star, 95 rooms. A very elegant, quiet hotel in lower part of village.
Novotel, Carretera de Mijas (tel: 48 58 61), 4-star, 130 rooms. One of the area's newest hotels, in a traditional Andalucian-style building. Good amenities here include a health centre.
Las Palmeras Sol, Paseo Marítimo s/n (tel: 47 27 00), 3-star, 424 rooms and apartments. A tall and spreading complex which like the other seafront hotels is much used by package holiday operators.
El Puerto Sol, Paseo Marítimo 32 (tel: 47 01 00), 317 rooms. A member of Spain's biggest hotel group, with standard accommodation and lots of amenities, including entertainment. Rooftop terrace and pool.
Pyr Fuengirola, Calle Lamo de Espinosa 6 (tel: 47 17 00), 3-star, 400 studio rooms. Big complex

Mijas, in the sierra foothills

overlooking the beachfront, with first-floor sun terrace and pool area.

Agur, Calle Tostón 4 (tel: 47 66 62), 2-star hostal, 30 rooms. Intimate and convenient for sea and town. Pleasant patio.

Sedeño, Calle Jacinto Benavente 1 (tel: 47 47 88), 2-star pension. Basic rooms, one street back from central seafront.

Nightlife

Fuengirola is more sedate than most of the coast's resorts. Most people soon find a place which for some reason special to them makes it their favourite night time haunt. There is certainly a fair choice of bars for quiet talking, bars with live or record music and bigger discos with louder music. **Galaxy** is the most exotic of these. In summer, there is quite a lively nightscene in the Puerto. Keep your eyes open for billboards, notices and handouts which advertise special events.

Restaurants

Simply walk along the Paseo Marítimo and the main road through Fuengirola, and take your pick from the menus displayed outside. Or do the same along Calles Cruz, Moncayo, España and other streets within the area bordered by Calles Jacinto Benavente and Matadero. In Mijas most of the eating places are close together in easy walking distance, and there is also a fair choice in urbanisations like Calahonda. These are some moderately priced favourites which are a little different or above the average of the many typical resort restaurants. Dinner

bookings are usually essential in the summer months.

La Baraka, Edificio Saturno, Paseo Marítimo (tel: 47 14 95). Provençal dishes including pizzas. The daily special is usually a good bet. Closed Wednesday in winter.

Portofino, Edificio Perla, Paseo Marítimo 29 (tel: 47 06 43). Near the Puerto on central beachfront, serving an Italian and international menu. Summer terrace; lunches from May to October. Closed Mondays.

The Raj, Calle Asturias 3 (tel: 46 94 70). Indian food: tandoori and all the usuals, well prepared and served in a pleasant ambience. Dinner only. Closed Thursdays.

La Langosta, Calle Francisco Cano s/n (tel: 47 50 49), on the corner with Calle Lope de Vega. International dinner menu on which seafoods predominate. Comfortable, long established and respected for fine food and good service.

Lew Hoad's Campo de Tenis, Carretera de Mijas (tel: 47 48 58). A sporty, friendly atmosphere, and the menu choice for lunch and dinner, inside or outdoors, is nicely balanced. Closed Mondays.

Valparaíso, Carretera de Mijas (tel: 48 59 75). A little pricier but worth it for a special occasion (the last night of your stay?) which Raffaele and Vittorio will make sure you enjoy in their elegant place. Refined presentation and service of international dinner menu. Dancing; closed Sundays.

Hostal Mirlo Blanco, Plaza de la Constitución, Mijas (tel: 48 57 00). Small choice of

Spanish and Basque dishes, well prepared and priced. The summer terrace overlooks the village's prettiest plazas.
Mijas Playa, La Cala, Mijas-Costa (tel: 48 55 81 or 49 37 49). On the seafront, with a good choice of international dishes, among which whole leg of lamb is a speciality. Dinner only. Closed Sundays.

Shopping
The fleamarket near the Fuengirola bullring on Tuesday mornings is the biggest along the coast. It is acceptable to bargain a bit, but not too insistently. If you are cooking for yourself, use the weekday food markets in Fuengirola and Mijas. Two hypermarkets off the N340 bypass have food, household goods and a wide range of other items.
Although there is a variety of good shops in the town centre, you will have a wider choice in Marbella and Málaga for instance. Plenty of places in Mijas are stacked with garish souvenirs and overpriced items you could buy almost anywhere, but among them are shops selling local craft items such as carpets, wicker and esparto grass, embossed silverware and locally made honey.

Special Events
The **Feria del Rosario**, in early October, is a week-long celebration centred on the permanent fair precinct, Recinto Ferial, where *casetas* (clubhouses) of different associations line three parallel streets. During the fair they are open to the public for shows, drinking, eating and merrymaking. The event emulates the much bigger and more famous April Fair in Seville, and is one of the great celebrations in Andalucía.

Sports
Bowling alley Bowling Palmeras Center, Calle Martinez Catena.
Bowls Rivera del Sol, Urbanización Miraflores, Mijas-Costa (tel: 83 32 40).
Golf You might try at the premier club, **Mijas Golf** (tel: 47 29 12 office, 47 01 66 clubhouse), which has two 18-hole courses designed by Robert Trent Jones.
Horseriding Centro Ecuestre Club del Sol, Sitio de Calahonda, Mijas-Costa; Rancho el Cañaón, Camino de Coin, near Mijas Golf.
Spectator sports Polideportivo Elola, Calle Menorca, is the venue for different sports.
Tennis Lew Hoad's Campo de Tenis, Carretera Mijas (tel: 47 48 58); Club del Sol, Sitio de Calahonda, Mijas-Costa (tel: 83 08 30); Tenis Center Aquarius, Urbanización Rivera del Sol, Mijas-Costa (tel: 83 39 40). Instruction and other facilities are offered.
Watersports During the main season, a choice of places along the beach offer equipment rental and instruction in board sailing and other watersports. Club El Océano, Torrenueva Playa, Mijas-Costa (tel 49 33 25), is a well-run health and leisure centre for all ages, right on the beach. Dinghy and boardsailing, waterskiing, a gymnasium, sauna, jacuzzi and steam room are among the amenities.

MARBELLA AND SAN PEDRO DE ALCÁNTARA

Calle San Cristobal, in Marbella's old town

Most of the main road running through Marbella is named Avenida de Ricardo Soriano, after a Spanish *marqués* who was the first to promote the town's virtues as a resort to his high-society family and friends. A nephew, Prince Alfonso von Hohenlohe of Liechtenstein, bought a small beachside farm just west of the town, which was then living off iron mining and fishing. He built a few chalets and began developing luxuriant gardens. In 1953 it opened as the Marbella Club and the 30-year-old prince's friends started coming to stay, play and party. Marbella became an 'in' place for a fair clutch of the rich, famous and titled, and so it has remained, though not without dramatic changes.

Its resident population is now estimated to be in excess of 80,000 people, with a large floating population which spends part of the year here. Additionally there is the larger annual influx of visitors coming for a few days or weeks. The Marbella Club Hotel, still a unique creation at the epicentre of the town's high life, is challenged by other top-rated places to stay. Many of the rich, famous and furtive now have their own luxury homes. Urbanisations with apartments and villas have spread across the land between sea and mountain on either side of the 16 miles (26km) of the N340 highway within the municipal limits – an area which includes San Pedro de Alcántara, or San Pedro. More and more pockets of barren land have been turned into golf courses and are carefully tended to remain a rich green throughout the year. All trace of the iron mining industry has gone: the mines, furnaces and port. There is a new fishing port, but fewer and fewer fish. There are also three marinas packed with luxury cruisers and yachts. The old town has been renovated without spoiling it, and is now more comfortable for its inhabitants and more attractive for visitors. It is packed with tempting shops and eating and drinking places. A new town has grown around it and runs down to the seashore and promenade. Thankfully, developers have showed, or have been made to show, more good taste than bad. High-class shops line the new streets, and in the town and the urbanisations, world-class restaurants and nightspots serve a demanding clientele. There are excellent facilities for sports, health care, recuperation and medical treatment. In three words much-vaunted by tourism promoters: Marbella is Marvellous. But there are a couple of provisoes: you need money to enjoy the very best of what Marbella offers, and it helps to have the right social connections. If you can do without the high life, it is

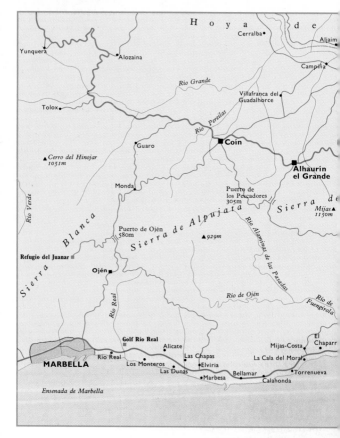

possible to have a good time without being rich. Both Marbella and San Pedro have places to stay, eat, drink or be entertained which do not demand a small fortune. The beaches are free, some sports and leisure amenities are not very costly, and it need cost very little to discover the many varied and wonderful places away from the coast – just get on a local bus.

Most visitors enter Marbella from the east, and on this edge of the resort is the Puerto Cabo Pino, the newest of Marbella's marinas. The complex of buildings in attractive and colourful pueblo style has apartments, shops, bars and restaurants, making it a self-contained enclave. Next along is Las Dunas, with a long stretch of beach backed by low dunes and a wooded area. A

**COSTA DEL SOL:
MARBELLA-MÁLAGA**

MARBELLA AND SAN PEDRO

string of urbanisations such as Hacienda Las Chapas, Marbesa and Elviria around here is followed by the Don Carlos and Los Monteros hotels (both 5-star and with extensive grounds), and the new Marbella Golf Course. After that comes the Golf Río Real course, and then the town outskirts. After about two miles (3km) through the town, the 'Golden Mile' begins – a stretch of densely concentrated luxury development, including the top hotels of Marbella Club, Puente Romano and Coral Beach. After Marbella centre, on the banks of the Río Verde, is the La Dama de Noche golf course. Next comes Puerto Banús, where people from all along the Costa del Sol arrive to gawp at the world's rich and their luxury yachts (which seldom leave the port). The first of Spain's pueblo-style marina developments has apartments, many shops and a big choice of places for drinks, food and entertainment, with new luxury complexes adjacent. The extensive urbanisation of Nueva Andalucía lies inland, with the golf courses of Los Naranjos, Las Brisas, Aloha and the new La Quinta. Behind rises the Sierra Blanca, which helps to give the area its mild winter climate. San Pedro follows, a little slower paced and with an undeveloped beach area backed by groves of eucalyptus trees (though a new sports-port is planned). The Río Guadalmina, and two golf courses and urbanisations of the same name, are at the municipal boundary with Estepona.

WHAT TO SEE

The area has witnessed the passing or settling of different peoples, and there have been some valuable archaeological discoveries locally, but Marbella is short of 'sights' – the main attraction is the way of life.
In the new part of the town, the park areas of La Constitución and La Alameda are attractive. The promenade, Puerto Deportivo, Puerto Pesquero and the *molas* protecting the beaches are other places of interest for a stroll. Otherwise, most sightseeing can be done on a short wander in the older quarter of Marbella.

◆◆◆
MARBELLA (OLD TOWN)

Marbella's old town is a warren of narrow streets and remnants of fortifications built by Moors, who held the town until 1485. There are also a few churches and public buildings built after that date. An easy stroll will reveal the changing styles: Moorish in the Casa del Corregidor (although it carries the later date of 1552); late Gothic and baroque respectively in the hospitals of San Juan de Dios and Bazán; Renaissance in the fountain on Plaza de Naranjos. The 'Orange Tree Square' has for long been the centre of the old town's life. It is where the intriguing assortment of people attracted to Marbella parades and poses, to see and be seen. The small chapel of Santiago dates from the 15th century; the main church, La Encarnación, is dated 1505. The Bazán hospital building is being converted to become the

Casa de Cultura, which will host exhibitions and other cultural events. Apart from the commercial art galleries, there are often shows of painting, sculpture, photography and other creative work in the Sala Municipal de Expociones, Calle Huerta Chica, and in many of the top hotels.

Accommodation

This is a small selection of hotels, tourist apartments (AT) and hostals, from a good range of places with high standards.

In Marbella town

El Fuerte, Avenida del Fuerte s/n (tel: 77 15 00, fax: 82 44 11), 4-star, 500 capacity. The best of the hotels in town faces Playa de la Bajadilla. The pool and terrace area is surrounded by gardens.

Jardines del Mar, Paraje Don Pepe 4 (tel: 77 60 00, telex: 79651), 3-key AT. On the western edge of town and only a short walk from the centre, this well-run and attractive apartment complex is set in luxuriant gardens. Two-room apartments are spacious and very comfortable. Good value.

Lima, Avenida Antonio Belón 2 (tel: 77 05 00), 2-star hostal, 124 capacity. Large bedrooms in a residential area near seafront.

El Castillo, Plaza de San Bernabé 2 (tel: 77 17 39), 2-star hostal, 40 capacity. Simple rooms in the old town, popular with young people.

La Pilarica, San Cristóbal 31 (tel: 77 42 52), 1-star hostal, 22 capacity. Impeccable hostal with comfortable rooms.

Seeking shade in the Plaza de Africa

East of Marbella

Incosol, Golf Río Real, N340 (tel: 77 37 00, fax: 82 31 78), 5-star, 400 capacity. Spa hotel with resident medical team, three heated pools, fitness and beauty treatments, leisure programmes and sports facilities.

Los Monteros, N340 (tel: 77 17 00), fax: 82 58 46), 5-star Gran Lujo, 337 capacity. Pine woods and tropical gardens surround this prestigious hotel which has excellent amenities for golf, tennis, horseriding and pure indulgence, at La Cabana beach club, other bars, two restaurants and night club.

Puerto Cabo Pino, N340 (tel: 83 17 10, telex: 77381), 3-key AT. Apartments for two, four, five and eight persons. Comfortable and situated right there at the heart of the Puerto's activities and amenities.

West of Marbella
Puente Romano, N340 (tel: 77 01 00, fax: 77 57 66), 5-star Gran Lujo, 392 capacity. The Marbella Club Hotel's new and bigger sister has followed its standards and is a pueblo-style complex, set in luxuriant gardens with much running water, spanned in one place by a small Roman bridge. Excellent amenities include a choice of restaurants, beach club with imported sand, health and fitness treatments, Manolo Santana Tennis Centre and Olivia Valère disco club.

Marbella Club Hotel, N340 (tel: 77 13 00, fax: 82 98 84), 4-star, 168 capacity. Forget about its mere 4-star rating – this is *the* place to stay. Luxurious rooms and bungalows are spread around mature gardens, and service is discreet but superb. Many guests find the environment so relaxing and pampering that they hardly leave it during their stay in Marbella. Beach club, grand lunch buffet, tennis, watersports and so on.

Cortijo Blanco, N340, San Pedro de Alcantara (tel: 78 09 00), 3-star, 219 capacity. Rustically furnished rooms face gardens, patios and pool. The hotel is a favourite of young couples with children.

El Cid, Extramadura 11, San Pedro de Alcantara (tel: 78 06 39), 2-star hostal, 50 capacity. An unpretentious place with unpretentious prices.

Avenida, Las Margaritas 19, San Pedro de Alcantara (tel: 78 31 92), 1-star pension. 22 capacity. Intimate, friendly, comfortable and cheap.

The Marbella Club Hotel is the first and last word in luxury

Nightlife

Much of Marbella's nightlife is invisible to the short-term visitor. It goes on behind the high walls of secure villas, between which different social sets do their nocturnal perambulations, often a continuation of the daytime partying around a huge private swimming pool. Catering firms do a roaring trade in Marbella. Most people soon find their own favourite place with some live or recorded music, and tend to return there. You should find plenty of choice if you walk the streets of the old town, or along and around Calle Camilo José Cela in the western part of the new district. Or go to Puerto Banús where there is a big choice of nightspots along and near the front, and in adjoining Benabolá. The **Salduba Pub** is in a good position for observing the port scene.

Three exclusive nightspots are **La Notte**, the piano bar adjoining Restaurante La Meridiana, where a singer often croons away the evening; **Olivia Valère**, the nightclub and disco in Hotel Puente Romano; and in summer only, the **Marbella Club Disco. Oh Marbella!** is a very animated summertime disco in the perfect setting of the Don Carlos Hotel Beach Club, N340. The **M25 Disco**, N340, has a reputation for unabandoned behaviour. Other evening entertainment includes flamenco, often arranged by hotels. **Ana Maria**, Plaza de Santo Cristo (tel: 77 56 46), offers a performance which mixes the authentic with jokes. **Cine Puerto Banús** shows films in Spanish and English. **Casino Nueva Andalucía**, N340, has French and American roulette, Solo O, Black Jack, Point and Bank, and Chemin de Fer from 20.00 to 05.00 hrs nightly (passport required). There is also a fruit machines hall, open from 18.00 hrs.

Ask at the tourist office and look for billboards and leaflets advertising special events. Big name stars give concerts in Marbella's open-air auditorium, football grounds or in Nueva Andalucía bullring.

Restaurants

Seek and you will surely find many places serving what you like at prices you are prepared to pay. In its eating places (and supermarkets, if you are cooking for yourself), Marbella satisfies a very cosmopolitan collection of visitors, not all of whom are millionaires.

Marbella's old town is a good place to look: try Calle Duque de Ahumada on the seafront and in back streets on the west side of Avenida de Miguel Cano. San Pedro's back streets have several restaurants as well. It is a case of looking at menus and making a choice, according to taste and pocket. As a last resort, there are the international franchises of Macdonalds, Burger King and Kentucky Fried along Avenida Ricardo Soriano.

There are over 200 restaurants, many of them very good, so this selection is just a sample, rather than a comprehensive survey. The excellence of the first three ensures their inclusion in any listing. By international standards they have a good quality-to-price ratio for a memorable dining experience. Menus change with the seasons, and all three have delightful summer terraces. Advance booking is usually essential.

La Hacienda, Urbanización Hacienda Las Chapas, N340 (tel: 83 12 67). Paul Schiff's acclaimed restaurant has the atmosphere of a large private villa, and has been a member of Relais y Chateaux since 1979. Schiff presents a personalised version of modern French and Spanish cuisine, inspired by a traditional training and long experience of catering. The gastronomic menu of five courses is excellent value. Dinner only in the summer. Closed Mondays.

Marbella Club Hotel, N340 (tel: 77 13 00). In a spacious room where the service is discreet but ever attentive, the conversation hums quietly as eyes rove on a 'personality' hunt. The menu is carefully created for international tastes. A member of Relais y Chateaux.

La Meridiana, Camino de la Cruz s/n, Urbanización Las Lomas de Marbella, N340 (tel: 77 61 90). A place of striking modern design in which to experience inventive modern Mediterranean cooking. The menu is created by owner Paolo Guirelli, whose personal direction is evident in the high standards. Dinner only in the summer. Closed Thursdays.

Gran Marisquería Santiago, Duque de Ahumada 50 (tel: 77 00 78). The best specialist seafood restaurant along the seafront is very popular with local people. If the price does not stagger you, try the *langosta*. Other dishes are moderately priced.

Koji, Edificio Fontanilla Azul, Calle Ramón Gómez de la Serra (tel: 77 51 86). Japanese cuisine for a discerning clientele. Prices are moderate. Closed Sundays.

El Meson del Pasaje, Calle Pasaje 5 (tel: 77 12 61). A choice of well-priced dishes from an international menu is available in the upstairs dining room of this traditional restaurant in the old town. Closed Thursdays.

Copperfields, Plaza Juan de la Rosa (tel: 82 05 42). Tony and June Randles provide excellent value and home cooking of English favourites in their intimate bar bistro.

La Posada, Calle San Juan de Dios 4. Also known as *Patio Andaluz*. The Jiménex family offers basic local fare and basic prices in a quaint setting.

West of Marbella

Don Leone, Puerto Banús (tel: 81 17 16). Quality cooking of all the Italian favourites at moderate prices in a pleasant, well-run, central restaurant. Terrace. Dinner only in the summer.

El Leon de Oro, Puerto Banús (tel: 81 50 44). Perhaps the choice of Chinese dishes is a bit overpriced, but then this is Puerto Banús. Good service, good view.

East of Marbella

Harbour Lights, Puerto Cabo Pino (tel: 83 74 83). A young team runs this bright and airy eatery serving local and English dishes at fair prices.

Out of town

Venta de Alcuzcuz, C339 San

Pedro to Ronda (tel: 78 19 89).
Very popular rural place,
especially with locals for Sunday
lunch. Concentrates on meats
and game prepared in Spanish
styles. Closed Mondays.
Refugio de Juanar, off C337
Marbella to Ojén (tel: 88 10 00).
The short menu of meat, poultry
and game dishes is cooked in
country style in this rustic
hostelry, a world away from
Marbella but only 30 minutes'
drive.

Shopping

As a place where enormous
wealth is concentrated and
displayed, Marbella has many
high-quality shops for fashions,
jewellery, designer items for the
home and the latest consumer
goods. Lack of competition
means that prices tend to be
higher than in Spain's big cities,
even for identical goods. It is
best to look for things which you
think you will not get elsewhere,
such as local arts and crafts.

There are quite a number of art
galleries, antique specialists
and craft shops, and the studios
of artists and sculptors can be
visited by prior arrangement
(get details at the tourist office).
Most of the best shopping can
be found as you wander through
the old town and along both
sides of Avenida Ricardo
Soriano, as well as in the streets
to the south, Avenidas de
Miguel Cano, Antonio Belón and
Calle Virgen del Pilar. The
Marbell Center, Avenida Ramón
y Cajal 12, has all sorts of small
shops and a supermarket. In the
back streets of Puerto Banús
there are more boutiques and
shops for jewellery, other
fashion accessories, art and gift
items. Near by is the big new
Christamar commercial centre,
and across the N340, the Centro
Plaza shopping centre of Nueva
Andalucía. On Saturday

*Puerto Cabo Pino, where the mountains
of apartments go down to the sea*

mornings a small antiques market is held around the bullring here. Weekly fleamarkets are held around Marbella's football stadium on Mondays and in Avenida Príncipe de Asturias, San Pedro, on Thursdays. All market times are 09.00 to 14.00 hrs.

If you are cooking for yourself, there are markets for fresh foods on weekdays on the corner of Calles Jacinto Benavente and Francisco de Quevedo in Marbella and in San Pedro's Plaza de Mercado. Hiper-Marbella, off the main road on Marbella's western outskirts, is well stocked with foodstuffs, household goods and consumer items.

Special Events

Marbella's patron saint, **San Bernabé**, is commemorated with a week's celebrations in early or mid June. **San Pedro**, patron saint of the village, has his day on 19 October, which is preceded and followed by days and nights of lively and very colourful celebrations.

Sports

Top hotels have good facilities or arrangements with other venues for golf, tennis or paddle tennis, horseriding and watersports.

Bowling alleys Bolera Axier, Plaza de los Olivos, Marbella; Bolera San Pedro, Calle Doctor Eusebio Ramírez, San Pedro.
Bowls Aloha Superbowl, Calle 1D, Nueva Andalucía (tel: 81 33 92).
Golf If you want to play on the oldest course, amid hills and palm trees, try for a game at Golf Río Real, N340 (tel: 77 37 76).

Horseriding Centro de Equitación Lakeview, Pantano Rota, San Pedro (tel: 78 69 34); Club Hípico Elviria, El Platero, Urbanización Elviria (tel: 83 52 72); Club Hípico Marbella, Urbanización Hacienda Cortés (tel: 77 05 39); Los Monteros Escuela de Equitación, Golf Río Real (tel: 77 06 75).
Sailing For up-to-date information and availability of charters, contact the Public Relations Officer at the marinas: Cabo Pino (tel: 83 15 37); Marbella (tel: 82 44 62); Puerto Banús (tel: 81 47 50).
Spectator sports The main ones are soccer, basketball and tennis competitions at municipal *polideportivos* or stadiums, and club venues. Enquire at tourist offices.
Squash Hotels Los Monteros and El Fuerte (see **Accommodation**).
Tennis Quite a few hotels have courts. Good instruction and extensive facilities are available at Hotels Puente Romano and Los Monteros (see **Accommodation**). There are two centres in the area of El Madroñal, off the C339 to Ronda: El Balcón de Tenis (tel: 81 20 69) and El Madroñal (tel: 78 09 90).
Watersports In seasons other than winter, various places on beaches offer gear rental and instruction in board sailing and other watersports. It is a case of looking for a set up which you like. Amenities are also available at the beach clubs of the smart hotels, among which those of Hotel Don Carlos (tel: 83 19 40) are highly rated by enthusiasts.

ESTEPONA

The simple elegance of Estepona

Local authorities and promoters call Estepona 'The Last Paradise' – an exaggeration maybe, but you can see their point. This is a working town in a delightful location, which has been less changed by tourist and residential development than the other main towns of the western Costa del Sol. The monument to workers, on the Paseo Marítimo, bears statues of a farmer and a fisherman, and these still seem more

appropriate than a building worker or hotel waiter. The town's saint is San Isidro Labrador, patron of farmers, and his feast day is enthusiastically celebrated. Unlike the other coastal towns, Estepona still considers agriculture very important to the economy, and there are Town Hall initiatives, such as introducing new crops, grants, quality control and better marketing. The fishing fleet remains active too. Estepona does cater for tourists, however, and looks set to develop this side of its economy further. In the summer of 1990 the town heard that it had inherited huge tracts of land with a value estimated between 30 and 60,000 million pesetas. Some of this has been sold to developers, to the chagrin of farmers who have paid to work the land for many decades. The debate as to the best use of the windfall goes on.

In all more than 50 urbanisations and tourist complexes have been developed or are still being built upon. They are mostly low-rise and on the seaward side of the 14-mile (23km) stretch of the N340 highway within Estepona's municipal limits. Among them is Costa Natura, Spain's first 'village' for nudists. Estepona's hotels only have around 1,700 beds, so it is in the complexes that the great majority of visitors stay – in the high season, visitors sometimes triple the resident population of 25,000.

Attracting golfers throughout the year is one of the main objectives of the authorities and developers, as elsewhere along the coast, and Montemayor will be Estepona's fifth golf club. The attractions of nearby Cádiz province and Gibraltar are also part of the town's appeal.

So as to see what makes Estepona different from the other main resort towns on the western side of the Costa del Sol, you should walk, ride or drive into the intensively farmed areas between the town and the rising ground up to the Sierra

Bermeja. Here you will find farmers working their farms, which average just 2.5 acres (1 hectare), using both the most ancient and simple methods, and the most modern. Lemons, the previous mainstay, are being replaced by more profitable avocados, mangoes, chirimoyas and other fruits in what is fast becoming a sub-tropical landscape. Further inland, you will come across many herds of goats. Their rearing and the production of cheese from their milk is increasingly important.

WHAT TO SEE IN AND AROUND ESTEPONA

◆◆◆
ESTEPONA (OLD TOWN)

A wander through the old part of town, between Calle La Terraza and Avenida de San Lorenzo, will reveal a lot of charm: narrow streets of whitewashed buildings with flower-decked balconies, *rejas* (grills) over windows, bright doorways and street names in ceramic tiles. The pretty, 18th-century Plaza de las Flores is appropriately usually bright with blooms, and the old Hospital de la Caridad, now the Casa de Cultura, has become an active focus of local cultural activity. Look out for the Torre del Reloj (clocktower), remnant of a 15th-century church; and for nearby Plaza del Rejoj, Plaza Blas Infante, and Plaza de San Francisco, dominated by the main church of Los Remedios (18th century). Along Calle Castillo are remains of the 15th-century walls of a castle which was originally built by the Moors.

◆◆
PUERTO DE ESTEPONA
To the west of the town, this is another place for a short wander to see the activity of both the sports and fishing harbours. Sit at one of the outdoor restaurants or cafés to watch and become part of the scene.

◆◆
PUERTO DUQUESA
eight miles (13km) west
Like Puerto de Estepona, this is a place to stroll around, sit at an outdoor café and absorb the atmosphere. Just beyond it on the shore is the Castillo de Sabinillas, built in the 17th century to protect the coast from Berber pirates. A bit further on lies Cádiz province and its many attractions, including the exclusive urbanisation of Sotogrande and the sparkling new Puerto Sotogrande.

Flowers on balconies are typical

◆◆
SIERRA BERMEJA
A short journey from the coastal strip takes you into a totally different landscape. Nine miles (15km) along the road to Jubrique is a turnoff into the woods of the Sierra Bermeja mountain range. The *pinsapo* fir grows on the higher slopes (follow a signed path to get there) and streams run through wooded glades inhabited by a variety of wildlife, of which you may catch glimpses. From the highest point, Alto Los Reales, 4,753 feet (1,449m), North Africa can be seen on a clear day.

Accommodation
This is a selection of hotels, tourist apartments (AT) and hostals to show the range – the full choice is much bigger.

Estepona
If you do not mind living above the busy Avenida de España, there are three hotels or hostals to consider. First choice should be:
Buenavista, Avenida de España

180 (tel: 80 01 37), 2-star hostal, 30 rooms. Simple and well-run, its room terraces overlook central beach area.
Caracas, Avenida San Lorenzo 32 (tel; 80 08 00), 2-star, 30 rooms. In a quiet quarter, it is plain, neat and comfortable.
Pilar, Plaza de las Flores (tel: 80 00 18), 1-star hostal, 10 rooms. Small, simple rooms, but the location on a pretty square is the best in town.

East of Estepona
Atalaya Park, N340 (tel: 78 13 00), 3-star, 448 rooms. Two blocks are set in spacious gardens facing a beach – only one among the many leisure and sports amenities on offer.
Santa Marta, N340 (tel: 78 07 16), 3-star, 12 rooms and 22 garden bungalows. There is nothing fancy here, but it is comfortable and on the beach.
Stakis-Paraiso, N340 (tel: 78 30 00), 3-star, 200 rooms. On rising ground about a mile (1.5km) from the beach (minibus) and next to El Paraiso Golf. Other good sports facilities are also available. Bedrooms and bathrooms are big.
El Pirata, N340 (tel: 80 12 90), 2-star AT. Blocks of comfortable bungalows, for two, three, four or five, in gardens at the seaside. Jolly Roger, El Galeón and El Pirata eateries.

West of Estepona
Costa Natura, N340 (tel: 80 15 00), 3-star AT. Naturist complex with apartments, for two, four, five and six, set in pleasant gardens and all facing the sea. Comprehensive sports and leisure amenities are offered.

COSTA DEL SOL: WEST

Nightlife
Nocturnal life is mostly concentrated on the port, but you may find your own favourite place in the old town or on one of the urbanisations. Some hotels and tourist complexes arrange entertainment. Many people make the trip to livelier, more fashionable Puerto Banús or Marbella town. **Delfos**, Calle Caridad 93, is the most popular young crowd disco in the town; **Riviera Club**, N340, has a more mixed crowd. Flamenco is staged at various venues. Ask at the tourist office.

Puerto de Estepona's fishing fleet

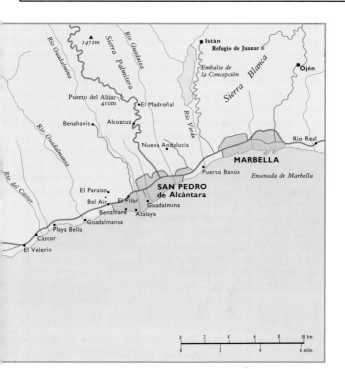

Restaurants

There is a good choice of places and price brackets. A wander around the back streets of the old town, or newer parts where working people live, will reveal simple places serving local fare at low prices. Many restaurants are only open for dinner. It is wise to telephone ahead. The following are all moderately priced except where stated.

Estepona

Costa del Sol, Calle San Roque (tel: 80 11 01). Behind the bus station, this unpretentious place is open for lunch, and has one of the best price-to-quality ratios on the coast for its French menu. The 'gastronomic menu' offers a taste of the best of the

Sea-bound or sky-bound, the quay at Puerto de Estepona has it all

day. Vegetarian and children's menus are also available. Closed Thursdays.

La Casa de mi Abuela, Calle Caridad 54 (tel: 79 19 67). In 'My Grandmother's House' they know how to treat and grill quality meats 'like the Gauchos eat in the Pampa'. Pricey but good. Closed Mondays.

La Fuente, Calle San Antonio 48 (tel: 79 29 79). A cosy place with a pleasant patio, serving a wide choice of international dishes. Closed Tuesdays.

La Pulga Que Tose, Pozo Pila 19 (tel: 80 27 49). 'The Coughing Flea' is an intimate restaurant which pays close attention to detail in its preparation and service of French and Belgian cuisine. Closed Sundays and Mondays.

Mesón Arni, Calle Mondéjar 16 (tel: 80 07 31). A wood-fired oven is used to cook the specialities of barbecued spare ribs and hot Mexican dishes in this rustic old town house. Closed Wednesdays.

Puerto de Estepona

El Cenachero (tel: 80 14 42). Serves Spanish favourites which are popular with local people, in a dining room or on the terrace (favoured by business people for their lunches). Closed Tuesdays.

El Puerto (no telephone). Owner-chef José Espigato presents local produce in a variety of other national cooking styles, to be enjoyed indoors or on the portside terrace. Closed Mondays.

East of Estepona

El Cid, Urbanización El Pilar, N340 (tel: 78 06 39). Roast lamb, steaks, lobster and paella are specialities in this popular English-run restaurant. Closed Sundays.

Mandarin Palace, Urbanización El Paraiso, N340 (tel: 78 38 23). Mr Chang is keen to please and offers a long and detailed menu of Chinese dishes in his spacious restaurant. Open daily for lunch and dinner.

Tres Leones, Avenida Gómez Barrios 1 (Bel Air) N340 (tel: 78 10 81). Thai food for lunch or dinner in a quiet, relaxing ambience. Closed Tuesdays.

West of Estepona

Bahía Beach, Urbanización Bahía Dorada, N340 (tel: 78 80 34).

Miguel Martos Martin is a supporter of the Friends of Andalucian Cuisine association, and their standards show in his restaurant. Closed Mondays.

Casa Celestino, Urbanización Arena Beach, N340 (tel: 80 25 42). Decorated as an Andalucian patio filled with plants, Casa Celestino has a regular following. The short lunch and dinner menu is especially good for fish. Closed Tuesdays.

Inland

Venta Los Reales, Carretera Jubrique (tel: 80 26 46). Country cooking in rustic, rural setting. Open daily for lunch and dinner; good prices.

Shopping

Do a window shopping tour of the old town to see the choice in boutiques and small craft and speciality shops before deciding what to buy. Quite a few foreign craftspeople have settled in the area and the Town Hall is encouraging local people to take up craftwork. The Sunday morning market in Puerto de Estepona is a good place to find crafts, household goods and the usual fleamarket things. From Monday to Saturday mornings there is a food market in Calle de la Villa. Hipersol, on the town's western edge, stocks foodstuffs, household items and consumer goods.

Special Events

Estepona has more celebrations than the other coastal towns. The first fortnight of May has the **Fiesta de la Santa Cruz**, starting with a procession on the 3rd and nightly merrymaking until the **Fiesta de San Isidro Labrador**, when the accent is on farming and the town is decorated with branches, fruit and flowers. The **Fiestas Mayores** take up the first week of July with sports, cultural events, processions, music, flamenco and fireworks. The **Día del Turista** on 15 September is celebrated with a huge beach party, competitions and music, when locals and visitors are all welcome to come along and join together in the fun.

Sports

Comprehensive sports facilities are available at Hotels Stakis-Paraiso and Atalaya Park. Another place which offers a lot is:

Club Leisure Sport, Urbanización Benamara, N340 (tel: 78 40 87). Tennis, paddle tennis, squash, swimming, aerobics, Nautilus gymnasium, massage, physiotherapy, sauna, hydrospa, hairdressing, beauty salon, and crèche.

Bowls Benavista Bowls Club, El Pilar, N340.

Golf See **Sport** section at end of book.

Horseriding Club St George, N340 (tel: 80 26 42), but remember the club requires advance bookings.

Sailing Club Náutico, Puerto de Estepona (tel: 80 09 94).

Tennis and squash Benavista Tennis and Country Club, N340 (tel: 78 77 72), tennis and squash; Club de Tennis Bel Air, N340 (tel: 78 06 58), tennis and frontón.

Watersports The best facilities are those provided at Hotel Atalaya Park.

Excursions from the Costa del Sol

Holiday operators and local travel agents can provide information about organised tours to places of possible interest, including the great cities of Seville, Córdoba and Granada. Or you could make your own arrangements. Some suggestions are made here, but you could go further afield to Gibraltar; Tetuan and Tangier in Morocco; or Cádiz province, where the Costa de la Luz offers wide, white beaches. Cádiz itself is Europe's oldest continuously inhabited city, and Tarifa is a boardsailing mecca.

In the same province, Jerez is the centre of sherry production, horsebreeding and bull ranching. Granada Province has a dramatic coastline and the resorts of Almuñécar and Salobrena; Las Alpujarras, the last mountain hideaway of the Moors, almost lost in time; and Solynieve, Europe's most southerly ski resort – as well as Granada city (see below).

Inland Towns and Villages

◆
ALHAURÍN DE LA TORRE

The old town, based on one of the area's most ancient settlements, is now an enclave among spreading industrial, commercial and residential zones, including new urbanisations catering for residential tourism. The population is fast growing above the last census count of almost 12,000. Local legend has it that Caesar beheaded Pompey here. La Torre del Cante, held

Rolling farmland beyond the sierra

in July, is one of Spain's most important flamenco festivals.

◆◆
ÁLORA

The 'capital' of the fertile Río Guadalhorce valley has some 16,000 residents in its area. Álora's Moorish look has been reduced by the rising of taller buildings, but there are still remains of the Moors' fortress. The town has the distinction that its 17th-century church is the largest in Málaga province after the city's cathedral. Málaga's version of flamenco, *las malagueñas*, originated in Álora and the town hosts a flamenco festival in June.

Álora is the gateway to the spectacular Garganta del Chorro gorge. It is also a gateway to Málaga's lakeland, via the villages of Carratraca, where there is a sulphur spa, and Ardales, still very Moorish in its layout.

♦♦
BENAHAVÍS

A growing centre for residential tourism and a favourite excursion for lunch, Benahavís is only five miles (8km) inland from the N340 coastal highway. There are a number of foreign-owned restaurants and some interesting art and crafts places, as well as good scenery.

♦♦♦
CASARES

15 miles (25km) from Estepona
From a distance, perched on and tumbling down its rocky spur which is crowned by the ruins of a Moorish castle, this is one of the most attractive and most photographed villages in Spain. It is also among the most frequently visited from the

Costa del Sol. On the outskirts are a few shops selling crafts and souvenirs, as well as places where you can get food and drink while enjoying views of the village.

♦♦
COÍN

13 miles (20km) from Marbella
With 22,000 inhabitants, this is a busy market town encircled by a productive area for olives, cereals, citrus and other fruits. Terracing and irrigation networks are the handiwork of the Moors. Churches raised after the Christian Reconquest of 1485 show Renaissance and Mudéjar features. Social life is centred on the main street. Food specialities include *hervia* and *poncima*, salads which include bitter

oranges, and *olla podrida*,
literally 'rotten pot', a pork and
vegetable stew. Fairs with an
agricultural accent are held in
May and August, and an
international festival of folk
dances is held during the first
14 days of January.

◆◆ GAUCÍN

40 miles (64km) from Marbella
Viewed from the south, Gaucín
rises prettily above the
surrounding patchwork of fields.
Close to, the village of crowded,
whitewashed houses and narrow
lanes is equally attractive. From
the partially restored Castillo de
Aguila there are views to the

High in the Sierra Bermeja, Casares
clings to the hillside

coast and Gibraltar. The Fonda
Nacional has been used since
the early 19th century as a
stopover on the then-arduous
journey from the coast to Ronda,
especially by British travellers
from Gibraltar.

◆ ISTÁN

Only 11 miles (18km) inland from
Marbella lies another world: a
Moorish hamlet of narrow
streets, with a typical Andalucian
plaza, 17 fountains and the ruins
of a Moorish castle. On the way
there are views of the lake of La
Concepción.

◆◆ MONTES DE MÁLAGA

The 'Mountains of Málaga' is a
beautiful area to the north and
east of Málaga city and adjoining
La Axarquía on the east. The
grapes to make Málaga wine
are grown here, and the area is
home to the Andalucian
verdiales folk singing custom.
Almogía is the largest town on
the northwestern side,
Colmenar, the largest on the
northeast. Near to the latter is
Riogordo, which presents a
spectacular Passion Play at
Easter, in which 10 per cent of
the population takes part.

◆ OJÉN

Marbella is only five miles (8km)
away along a road through
woods and thickets. The village
was Moorish until an uprising in
1560, when the Moors fled to
Las Alpujarras in Granada, and
it has preserved much of its look
from that time. There are places
serving local fare on the
approach to the village.

EXCURSIONS

Larger Towns and Cities

◆◆◆
ANTEQUERA

28 miles (45km) from Málaga

The largest municipality in Málaga province has some 42,000 people, both in the town and in some twenty villages and hamlets, spread across the fertile *hoya* (vale) or in the surrounding mountains. Prehistoric monuments show Antequera's strategic importance, which was recognised by successive conquerors. The Romans left their mark and so did the Moors. Prince Fernando captured it in 1410 and it became a forward base for the long assault on Granada. There was a spree of building churches, convents, monasteries, fine civil buildings and noble palaces which has left the town with a rich legacy of Renaissance, Mudéjar and baroque buildings.

A good way to start looking around is to go up to the high ground on the town's southeastern edge. The **Alcazaba** was built by the Moors in the 14th century on the ruins of a Roman castle. The best feature of the remaining fortifications is the **Torre del Papabellotas** belfry tower. Below the Alcazaba is the big church of **Santa María la Mayor**, completed in 1550 and recently restored, which has an ornate façade and a sparse interior graced by Mudéjar ceilings. It faces a square and the **Arco de los Gigantes**, a construction of 1585, which frames a view of the town below. Looking east, the view is towards **La Peña de los Enamorados** (Lovers' Rock) from which two lovers, a Muslim and a Christian, are said to have jumped, in order to be together in death rather than apart in life. The **Museo Municipal**, in the 18th-century Palacio de Nájera, has one of the most beautiful bronze statues from Roman Spain yet discovered. *El Efebo* is the life-size figure of a boy, made in the first century and probably copied from a Greek work done 500 years earlier. The tourist office is in the same building. Near by are the 16th-century churches of **Encarnación**, with Mudéjar coffered ceilings, and **San Sebastián**, in Renaissance style with a baroque and Mudéjar tower. The **Palacio Consistorial** or Ayuntamiento (Town Hall) is a much- remodelled Franciscan monastery, with a cloister. Adjoining it is **Los Remedios**, a 17th-century church dedicated to Antequera's patron saint. Among the many other fine churches, the best are the **Convento de San Zoilo**, a late Gothic Franciscan monastery finished in 1515 and remodelled during the following century, and the **Iglesia del Carmen**, a Mudéjar structure completed in 1633. Like Santa María and Los Remedios, these are national monuments, as are the Moorish Alcazaba and the **Puerta de Málaga**.

The **Conjunto Dolmenico**, just on the town's eastern edge, comprises two stone tombs dating from around 2000BC. The one known as Menga is the biggest and best maintained of its type yet discovered anywhere. Built of 31 stone slabs hauled from elsewhere, some weighing 180 tons, it is 80 feet (25m) deep and 12 feet (3.75m) high. Viera is a smaller tomb of similar construction.

The **Parque Natural Torcal de Antequera**, eight miles (13km) south of the town, comprises 2,965 acres (1,200 hectares) of limestone formations shaped by wind and water into fantastic forms. Visitors follow marked paths, yellow for short and easy, or red for more difficult and longer.

Laguna de Fuente de Piedra, 14 miles (23km) northwest of the town, is the only place in the peninsula where a large colony of pink flamingoes regularly nests. Flocks of 15,000 birds usually arrive in April and stay until early September. The lagoon is also home to other bird species, reptiles and amphibians.

Antequera from the Alcazaba

EXCURSIONS

Antequera's prosperous plain

Accommodation

Although it justifies a longer stay, Antequera's visitors are usually daytrippers, so not much good accommodation has been built. An exception is:

Parador Nacional, García del Olmo s/n (tel: 84 00 61), 3-star, 55 rooms. Modern building in regional style, with spacious and comfortable public areas, bedrooms and bathrooms.

Restaurants

Porra, a cold vegetable and bread soup, is a speciality. Two good places at which to try regional cooking are the **Parador Nacional** (see Accommodation) and **Chaplin**, Calle San Agustín 3 (tel: 84 30 34).

Shopping

Articles made from esparto grass, woodwork, embroidery, silverwork and leatherwork are the local specialities. Calle Infante Don Fernando and streets to the north of it form the main shopping district. A fleamarket is held on Sunday in Avenida de la Estación.

Special Events

The **Feria** in August is the biggest local celebration.

whose variety and interest is being discovered by an increasing number of visitors. The city's greatest legacy is **La Mezquita**, the magnificent mosque which was begun in AD785 and reached its present great size by 990. It ranks among the world's finest buildings, and its *mihrab* (prayer niche) is a special gem. After taking the city in 1236, Christians removed some of the mosque's 856 interior columns, and during the 16th century they began building a Gothic **cathedral** within it. The cathedral took 243 years to complete, and acquired decoration in later styles.

The **Alcazar de los Reos Cristianos**, which was started in the 14th century as a palace of the Christian kings, has water gardens and wide views from its towers. The **Puente Romano** (Roman Bridge), first restored by the Moors and restored many times since, leads to the **Torre de la Calahorra**, a 14th-century guard tower where now a diorama and wax figures depict the life and history of Muslims, Jews and Christians in Córdoba and the rest of Andalucía. Downstream from the bridge are three Arab mills. In the oldest part of the city, narrow streets are lined by fine mansions and other buildings, whose *cancelas* (wrought-iron gates) lead to cool, beflowered patios where fountains play. This is **La Judería** quarter where the great Jewish scholar Maimónides was born and a synagogue of the 14th century has survived. Cervantes mentions the **Posada del Potro**

♦♦♦
CÓRDOBA
113 miles (182km) from Málaga
Córdoba has had a glorious past. Under the Romans it was the administrative city for the rich province of Baetica; under the Moors it became western Europe's biggest, most cultured city. Packed with monuments and echoes of the past, but in its own way living vibrantly in the present, this is a city which leaves an indelible mark in the memory.

Most of Córdoba sits on the Río Guadalquivir's northern bank, with mountains not far behind. It is the capital of a province

(Inn of the Colt) in *Don Quixote*. It is now an arts and crafts centre. The **Museo Municipal de Bellas Artes** has works by Córdoban artists and by the better-known Zurbaran, Goya and Murillo. The **Museo Julio Romero de Torres** takes its name from an artist who painted Córdoba and its women in the early part of this century, and is very popular. Wrought-iron balconies hang on the brick façades of the arcaded **Plaza de la Corredera**, built in the 17th century; in the handsome **Museo Arqueológico**, you can see a rich collection from prehistory to baroque. The **Palacio de los Marqueses de Viana** is a palatial town house with 14 patios. This beguiling city has many more museums, churches, streets, squares and monuments to intrigue and delight its visitors. Five and a half miles (9km) west of Córdoba is the **Medina Azahara**, built by Abderraman III as the world's most splendid palace-city. Its glory was brief, because it was sacked by Berber mercenaries in 1010 and for centuries its stones were used for building elsewhere. Partial restoration continues on the huge site.

Accommodation

Thanks to expectations of a deluge of visitors spilling over from Expo '92 in Seville, Córdoba has a number of quite new hotels. Three favourites are: **Meliá Córdoba**, Jardines de la Victoria (tel: 29 80 66), 4-star, 200 capacity. Good service and comfort in pleasant downtown location.
Parador Nacional, Avenida de la Arruzafa (tel: 27 59 00), 4-star, 188 capacity. Big rooms, gardens and pool in quiet residential area.
Maimónides, Calle Torrijos 4, (tel: 47 15 00), 3-star, 152 capacity. Close to the mosque and old quarter.

Restaurants

Be sure to try a glass of *fino* from Montilla, with which you will usually get a tapa. The best choice of eating places is found in the old quarter.
Confederación de Peñas, Calle Luque s/n. Simple food at low prices, inside or on the patio.
El Caballo Rojo, Calle Cardenal Herrero 28 (tel: 47 53 75). Regional dishes include Mozarabe specialities.

Shopping

Córdoba lends its name to *Cordobanes* leatherwork, and also produces jewellery and other works in silver and gold, pottery and guitars. In the Zoco, craftspeople have workshops around a courtyard. A lively 'allsorts' market is held daily in the Plaza de la Corredera.

Special Events

May is a month of continuous celebration: **Cruces de Mayo**, when decorated crosses adorn public places; **Romería de La Virgen de Linares** (a pilgrimage); the **Patio Competition** with many private patios opened for visits; and **international festival of theatre and dance**, hosted by the theatre at Italica. The two-yearly **Flamenco Festival** is held in even-numbered years, and an **international jazz festival** is held annually in November.

◆◆◆
GRANADA

79 miles (127km) from Málaga

Even if you make no other excursions from the Costa del Sol, you should not miss Granada. With its extraordinary past and flourishing present, it makes what for many is an ideal combination of old and new. Today it is busy with life as a market town and commercial city, but enlivened by being an important conference and cultural centre, and home of Spain's third largest university. Monuments, concerts, exhibitions, theatre and a lively nightlife cater to all tastes. Near by is the popular ski resort of Solynieve.

The town sprawls across three mountain spurs thrusting into a large and fertile plain, one of the richest farmlands in the country. Granada was occupied by both Romans and Visigoths, but rose to prominence with the Moors. During the 11th century it broke away from Córdoba's

Moorish citadel and palace, La Alhambra is a beacon for travellers to Granada

caliphacy to create its own kingdom, and under the Nasrid dynasty (1246–1492) the city developed into one of the most powerful and artistic centres of the Middle Ages.

The priority for most visitors is the sprawling, magical, Moorish palace of **La Alhambra**, where fine arabesque traceries, coloured mosaics, cool colonnades and sparkling fountains greet the wanderer at every turn. Delicate Nasrid architecture, stunning workmanship and sensitive restoration combine to make the Alhambra one of the most remarkable medieval Arab palaces in the world today. Beside it stands the contrastingly austere 16th-century **Palacio de Carlos V**. A little higher up the hill lies the summer palace of **El Generalife**, with its shady avenues, water

EXCURSIONS

gardens, fountains and airy gazebos.

Back in the town centre, visit the huge 16th-century **cathedral**. Next door is the richly decorated **royal chapel**, burial place of the Catholic Kings, with a wealth of carving and Italian, Flemish and Spanish paintings. Old Granada is best seen by following the **Carrera del Darro** where you will find the impressive **archaeological museum** and 11th-century **Moorish baths**. On the same side of the river are the twisted back streets of the **Albaicín** quarter. Hidden patios, shady flower gardens and lofty turrets adorn the mansion houses. A little further upstream is **Sacromonte**, the traditional home of cave dwelling gypsies.

Accommodation

The city offers a variety of good quality hotels, with many renovations and new constructions undertaken for the 1995 World Skiing Championships.

Close to the Alhambra:
Alhambra Palace, 2 Calle Peña Partida (tel: 22 14 68), 4-star. Mock-Moorish surroundings and panoramic views.
Parador Nacional de San Francisco (tel: 22 14 93), 4-star. Once a Franciscan convent, and considered by many to be the best parador in southern Spain. Book well in advance.
América, 53 Calle Real de la Alhambra (tel: 22 74 71), 1-star. Intimate atmosphere, though closed in winter.

Town centre
Luz Granada, 18 Avenida de la Constitución (tel: 20 40 61) and **Meliá Granada**, 7 Calle Angel Ganivet (tel: 22 74 00) supply traditional 4-star quality and services.

Restaurants

For a wide choice, look in the back streets around the cathedral, Plaza Bibarrambla and Plaza Nueva.
Los Leones, 10 Acera del Darro (tel: 25 50 07), is one of Granada's oldest establishments, offering traditional Andalucian cooking and Granadine specialities.
Sevilla, 12 Calle Oficios (tel: 22 12 23). Once a rendezvous for the poet Garcia Lorca, Manuel de Falla and other notables. Serves imaginative regional dishes and charcoal-cooked meats.

Shopping

Granada specialities are embroidery, lace, ceramics, copperwork and marquetry. You will also find carpets, rugs, guitars and leather goods. The Alcaicería, once the site of the old Moorish silk market, is today a modern precinct full of souvenirs and trinkets. The Corral de Carbón is an interesting crafts centre with a 14th-century façade. More antique and souvenir shops lie within the Alhambra palace complex.

Special Events

The **Holy Week** processions count among Spain's finest. During June and July the city hosts an **international festival of music and dance** in the Generalife and Palacio de Carlos V.

◆◆◆
RONDA

63 miles (102km) from Málaga
Ronda is perched high on a
ridge, with sheer cliffs dropping
away on three sides. It makes
an unforgettable sight from the
west, where you can see the
Puente Nuevo spanning the
deep Tajo gorge, with buildings
clinging to the chasm's edge.
The town is capital of the
surrounding hills and mountains,
where Paleolithic people once
lived and smuggling bandits
roamed until quite recently. Its
strategic position and the fertile
plains which stretch away from
the town made it attractive to a
succession of settlers. The
Celtiberians called it Arunda,
the Romans renamed it Munda.
The Moors brought it great
prosperity, but in 1485 they
were defeated by the
cannonballs and 38,000 troops of
the Marqués de Cádiz.
Most visitors arrive from the
south, passing through the old
town and crossing the Puente
Nuevo to the Plaza de España in
the new Mercadillo area, to
park near by or alight from a
coach. As you enter Ronda this
way, there are two gateways in
what remains of the walls:
Puerta de Carlos V, 16th-century
in Renaissance style; and **Puerta
de Almocabar**, 13th-century and
Moorish. It took from 1751 to
1793 to build the **Puente Nuevo**
(New Bridge), 314 feet (96m)
above the Tajo gorge at its
highest and narrowest point.
The architect fell to his death
from the basket lowering him on
an inspection of the work. Cross
the bridge (which has become
the city's symbol) to go back

*Puente Nuevo: new bridge to an old
town*

EXCURSIONS

into the old town, where most of the sights are.

Buildings along the cobbled streets feature window grills and other decorative wrought-iron work for which Ronda is well known. The **Casa de Modragón** is a town mansion with a Renaissance façade and Mudéjar interior features. Some archaeological finds are displayed. Facing the attractive **Plaza de la Ciudad** is **Santa María la Mayor**, originally a

Rooms with a view over the Tajo Gorge

mosque which the Catholic Kings converted, and which was partly rebuilt after an earthquake in 1580. It has Gothic, Renaissance and baroque elements, including a tower which was a minaret and now has a Renaissance belfry, and a balcony from which the aristocracy watched spectacles in the square. The **Casa del Rey Moro** is a 19th-century palace, with hanging gardens and a staircase cut into the rock. Called the **Mina de Ronda**, it leads to the river below, and in times of siege Christian slaves had to use it to carry water to their masters. The privately owned **Palacio del Marqués de Salvatierra** has a handsome Renaissance façade and a splendid balcony of wrought iron. Near by is the **Puerta Felipe V**, a gateway built in 1742. Down the slope, the **Puente Viejo**, a Roman bridge rebuilt in 1616, and the **Puente Arabe**, a restored Moorish bridge, cross the Río Guadalevin. The **Baños Arabes**, 13th-century Moorish baths, are being restored.

Ronda's **Plaza de Toros**, completed in 1785, is 210 feet (64m) wide and has fully covered seating. It was in this bullring that Pedro Romero (1754–1839) perfected the ritual of bullfighting on foot, so it is regarded as a sacred place by modern bullfighting enthusiasts. It has a bullfighting museum. Near by is the peaceful and shady park, **Alameda del Tajo**, offering spectacular views from its balcony to the gorge below, with the wide expanse of plains and mountains beyond. Walking

through the Mercadillo district will reveal a few more places of interest, besides the daily life of a busy inland town.

Northwest is **Ronda la Vieja** (Old Ronda), the site of Roman Acinipo, with a reconstructed theatre. Southwest is the **Cueva de Pileta**, where remarkable cave paintings have been found.

Accommodation

There are two low-priced hostals on Calle Cristal, numbers 7 and 11. For more upmarket accommodation, try: **Reina Victoria**, Calle Jerez 25 (tel: 87 12 40), 4-star, 162 capacity. Comfortable rooms overlooking peaceful gardens, with views to plains and mountains. Public rooms have early 19th-century elegance. **Polo**, Calle Mariano Soubiron 8 (tel: 87 24 47), 3-star, 60 capacity. Less grand but also comfortable and in the town centre.

Restaurants

The Ronda area is known for its good morcilla and chorizo sausages, *lomo* (loin of pork), and for *pestiños*, which are cakes made with oil.
Pedro Romero, Virgen de la Paz 18 (tel: 87 10 61). Opposite the bullring and full of bullfighting memorabilia, it is a touch touristy but offers *especialidades Rondeñas* and international dishes at moderate prices, plus good service.
Don Miguel, Villanueva 4 (tel: 87 10 90). Moderately priced Spanish dishes indoors or on the terrace, with views of Puente Nuevo. Closed Tuesday lunch and Sunday in summer, Tuesday night and Wednesday October to May.

EXCURSIONS

Seville's Plaza de Espana

Shopping

Ironwork, forged and sculpted, is Ronda's biggest speciality. Saddlery, reproduction and antique furniture are others. Look for craft shops in back streets. The pedestrianised Carrera Vicente Espinel, commonly known as Calle de la Bola, is the main shopping and strolling street. A Sunday market is held in the Barrio de San Francisco.

Special Events

The feast of the **Virgen de la Paz** is held on 24 and 25 January, followed by the **Fiestas de la Reconquista**, from 20 to 24 May, and the **Romería de la Virgen de la Cabeza**, on 14 June. The **Feria y Fiestas de Pedro Romero** are a celebration of the matador and of bullfighting, with picturesque costumes, from the end of August into September.

◆◆◆
SEVILLE

133 miles (214km) from Málaga
Capital of Andalucía, fourth largest city in Spain and once the fourth largest in the world, Seville is where many of the archetypal images of Spain and its people come alive. Here bullfighting and flamenco are popular passions, annual displays of great religious solemnity contrast with colourful frivolity, and the *mañana* syndrome is strong. The town is also a busy port, lying 71 miles (115km) from the sea on the Rio Guadalquivir.

Seville had its most glorious period when it held the monopoly of trade with the New World. The hosting of Expo '92 in Seville could be seen as a bid to make the city the centre of world attention once again.
Seville's **cathedral** is the third largest in the world, and was one of the last great Gothic edifices to be built. Inside, it drips with gold, other rich decoration and fine art. It was built on the site of a mosque, remains of which include the **Patio de los Naranjos**, the ritual ablution courtyard, and **La Giralda**. The latter was built in the 12th century, to be the most remarkable minaret in the Muslim world. Christians added the belltower and the bronze weathervane figure of Faith. Walk up the ramp inside the tower for a panoramic view across the city, and a better idea of the cathedral's massive size.
Several styles coexist in the **Reales Alcázares** (Royal Palace), but overall the effect is of a Moorish palace, much like

Granada's Alhambra. *Azulejos* (wall tiles) were brilliantly used in the decoration. In the shady and peaceful gardens, fountains play among ponds and orange groves. Adjoining the Reales Alcázares and gardens is the **Barrio de Santa Cruz**, including much of the old Jewish quarter. Tourists flock here to be delighted by narrow streets and small squares, pots of flowers, bowers of jasmine and many orange trees. Buildings range from picturesque to imposing, but common features include wrought-iron *rejas* (window grills), doors and balconies. Amongst them are bars, restaurants, art galleries and craft shops. At night, students in traditional dress serenade strollers and diners.

The **Casa de Pilatos** is the most outstanding example of many palaces dating from Seville's heyday. It is built and decorated in Mudéjar and Renaissance style, with a rich and varied collection of sculptures,

paintings and furnishings. The **Fabrica de los Tabacos**, second largest building in Spain, was completed in 1771 and now houses two faculties of Seville's university. The **Lonja** mercantile exchange, completed in 1598, serves as the Archivo de las Indias, in which four million documents relating to Spain's American connection are preserved. In the chapel of the 17th-century **Hospital de la Caridad** there are paintings by Murillo and Valdés Leal. More of their work and that of great masters like Velázquez (a Sevillano), El Greco and Goya can be seen in the **Museo de Bellas Artes**. A small maritime museum occupies the **Torre del Oro**, the riverside tower built by Seville's Almohade rulers in the 13th century.

From its staging of the Ibero–América Exhibition in 1929, Seville gained new buildings in and near the big

Eyecatching Seville from La Giralda

EXCURSIONS

Parque de Maria Luisa. The most impressive is the **Plaza de España**, with its semicircle of buildings now used as government offices. Pavilions in the park's Plaza de América now house two museums well worth visiting: the **Museo Arqueológico** and **Museo de Artes y Costumbres**.

For churches, convents and chapels, baroque is the prevalent style, but some also have Gothic, Mudéjar and Renaissance elements. A few notable examples are the churches of **Santa Ana** and **Santa María Magdalena**, and the convents of **Santa Paula** and **Santa Ana**.

Accommodation

Seville has several new hotels and apartments, thanks to Expo '92. Prices have risen sharply, however, and may remain high for some time. Visitors are advised to make advance enquiries at tourist offices and travel agents about current availability and prices, and to book before arrival. Not so much a mere hotel, more a grand old city institution, is:
Hotel Alfonso XIII, Calle San Fernando 2 (tel: 422 2850, fax: 421 6033), 5-star Gran Lujo, 280 capacity. Built for the 1929 exhibition, it is very formal and offers old-fashioned luxury at today's top prices.

Restaurants

El tapeo, moving from bar to bar to partake of tapas and a drink, is very much part of Seville's food and drink scene. So is going to a *cocederos* to buy *pescaíto frito*, fresh fish fried in olive oil.
Casa Robles, Calle Alvarez Quintero 58 (tel: 421 3150). Andaluz cuisine in a smart, typical Seville restaurant where prices are moderate.
Ega a-Oriza, Calle San Fernando 41 (tel: 422 7211). Basque and international cuisine in one of the city's most elegant restaurants. Closed Sundays.
El 3 de Oro, Calle Santa María de la Blanca 34. A variety of self-service dishes at budget prices. Closed Saturdays.

Shopping

Look out for ceramics, including decorative wall tiles; silver, gold and iron work; embroidery; leather clothing and other items; and flamenco accessories. At some convents, nuns sell sweet delicacies or embroidery. On weekdays, craft and jewellery stalls are set up in Plaza del Duque. A fleamarket is held on Thursday in Calle Feria. On Sundays another market for crafts, antiques, jewellery and the like is held in Alameda de Hércules.

Special Events

No other city surpasses Seville in its zealous display of deep devotion during the religious festivals of **Semana Santa** (Holy Week), **Corpus Christi** (May/June), **Romería del Rocio** (Whitsun) and the **Immaculate Conception** on 8 December. Contrasting with those is the self indulgence and gaiety of the week-long **Feria de Abril** celebration of spring. It is followed by **Cita de Sevilla**, a programme of cultural presentations through May and June. In July the **Feria de Mayo** includes shows, flamenco and bullfights.

PEACE AND QUIET

PEACE AND QUIET

Wildlife and Countryside on and around the Costa del Sol

by Paul Sterry

Most people think of the Costa del Sol as a region of sun, sand and tourist development. This is certainly true for many stretches of shoreline, but there are still areas of natural habitat left along parts of the coast, and by travelling inland for even a short distance, visitors can find a Spain virtually unspoilt and seemingly untouched by time. Summer visitors generally see a landscape of dry and brown vegetation, scorched by the Mediterranean sun. Come here in spring, however, and you will find it to be quite different: flowers grow in profusion, insect life is abundant and Mediterranean birds can be found almost everywhere. Although spring is undoubtedly

Broom in bloom on the maquis

the richest season, summer visitors can still find areas of interest by travelling away from the coast to such places as Serrania de Ronda.

The Coast

Although the waters of the Mediterranean are rich and full of life, little evidence of it can be found on the seashore. This is mainly due to the small tidal range, the sea being effectively land-locked. The result is that rock pools and mudflats are virtually unknown because low tide, such as it is, uncovers very little of the shore.

Birds will probably be the most exciting things seen from the coast. During the late winter and early spring, westerly gales in the Atlantic sometimes drive oceanic seabirds through the Straits of Gibraltar and into the western Mediterranean. These

PEACE AND QUIET

storm-driven waifs eventually make their way back to the open sea but if the winds are onshore, their passage sometimes brings them close to land. Species such as gannets, Wilson's petrels and little shearwaters have even been seen from beaches in Málaga during such weather conditions. However, more reliable seawatching can be had at Cabo de Gata, Cabo Sacratif and Pra del Sabinal.

Interest at sea is not entirely confined to birds. Common dolphins often feed in large groups around the Straits of Gibraltar and sometimes venture eastwards along the coast.

Bee-eater

Maquis

At one time, much of the western part of the Costa del Sol would have been cloaked in forest, comprising species such as evergreen oaks and aleppo pines. In many parts of the region, as well as the Mediterranean coast as a whole, the woods have long-since gone, being felled for firewood and timber, and cleared for farming. But natural regeneration of the vegetation has created a habitat known as *maquis* which is particularly noticeable between Gibraltar and Málaga, where the winter rainfall is generous compared to the eastern Costa del Sol. Maquis is characterised as much by smell as by appearance: fragrant and pungent herbs grow densely among low-growing bushes and shrubs. Conspicuous plants include species of thyme, rosemary, gorse, broom, heathers and asphodels as well as dwarf fan palms, olives, mastic trees and Kermes oak; the latter is recognised by its evergreen, holly-shaped leaves. Several species of cistuses can also be found; the flowers have the appearance of crêpe paper and, depending on the species, the leaves might be sticky, waxy or aromatic.

The birdlife of the maquis is varied. Most species are easiest to see early in the morning and in the spring, when males will be singing. Sardinian warblers, with neat black-and-white plumage and a conspicuous red eye-ring, are common, as are Dartford warblers and subalpine warblers.

A rich harvest of cork oak bark

Also look out for bee-eaters, hoopoes and woodchat shrikes. Although the latter species is a comparatively small, perching bird it behaves like a bird of prey: it waits on branches and fenceposts scanning the ground for insects and small lizards, which it fearlessly attacks.

Woodlands

Woodland is an unfamiliar sight along most of the Costa del Sol. But there are extensive cork oak woods north of Gibraltar, and on the higher elevations of many of the Sierras there are pine woods.

The bark of the cork oak is harvested at regular intervals and is a valuable crop in the Andalucian region. The ground flora beneath the trees is often rich, and butterflies such as fritillaries, cleopatras, swallowtails and two-tailed pashas can be found.

Birds also find the cork oak woods an attractive habitat.

Cork Oak
Cork oaks are a characteristic feature of many Andalucian hillsides, the thick fleshy bark being used to make corks for wine and sherry bottles. The first crop of cork is taken after about 15 years but its poor quality means that it can only be used for tanning. Thereafter, good quality cork is harvested every 15 to 20 years and most trees continue to be productive for at least 150 years.

Hoopoes nest in holes and cracks in the gnarled trees. Although rather secretive when nesting, they are often seen in flight, when the black-and-white wing pattern is conspicuous. Little owls also nest in holes and can sometimes be seen perched unobtrusively on branches during the daytime. Far less easy to spot is the Scop's owl, whose cryptic plumage renders it almost invisible. At night, however, its call – a loud and repetitive, sonar-like bleep – is often heard.

PEACE AND QUIET

Birthworts, or 'Dutchman's pipe'

Pine woods, if undisturbed, may develop a rich growth of plant life on the woodland floor. Tree heathers and cistuses flourish in glades and clearings and orchids can be abundant in the early spring. Serins sing from the higher branches and nightingales serenade the visitor from the tangled undergrowth. With luck and persistence, visitors may also find Orphean warblers, melodius warblers and olivaceous warblers as well. For the best areas of cork oak woodland, drive the roads inland from Estepona and south from Ronda. Pine forests can be seen on the Sierra Bermeja.

Spring Flowers
Although seemingly barren and lifeless during the long, hot summers, inland areas of the

Costa del Sol are green and full of life during the winter and spring. Although a few trees and shrubs are evergreen and can survive the summer drought, the growing period of most plants in the region is strongly linked to the seasonal rains.

From May until October, virtually no rain falls at all, but from October until March, life-giving water triggers new growth. There is considerable variation in the rainfall throughout the Costa del Sol: the western region receives four or five times as much annual rain (400–500mm per annum) as the eastern half, with most of it falling between December and February. The resulting difference in vegetation is striking between west and east, the latter being distinctly more barren and stony in appearance even in winter.

Although some of the region's spring flowers appear annually from seeds, many survive the summer drought in the form of underground bulbs or tubers. They begin to grow when the first rains appear in autumn, and by early spring squills, irises, asphodels, narcissi and crocuses are in bloom.

Open ground and fields are good places to look for many of the seasonal plants of the Costa del Sol. Among the more characteristic are mallows, mallow-leaved bindweed, borages, birthworts, buttercups, and salvias. Maquis vegetation is generally more colourful and productive for the plant hunter, and rock roses, several species of cistuses and spiny members of the pea family can be found. By driving away from the coast and into the hills and mountains that back on to the Costa del Sol, visitors can find plants in flower later in the year than would be the case in the lowlands. Although the spring is undoubtedly the time of year to visit the Costa del Sol for flowers, a second flush of autumn species also appears in September and October. Many of these also survive as bulbs and tubers during the drought, and autumn squill, sea squill and autumn snowflake are characteristic.

Bird Migration

Many of the birds that breed in Europe are only summer visitors to the region. In autumn, millions of birds migrate south to Africa to escape the harsh European winters and to find better feeding. Each spring, they make the return journey, returning to their breeding grounds and timing their arrival and nesting to coincide with the fresh growth of plant life and renewed insect abundance. On their migration, one major natural obstacle stands between Europe and Africa – the Mediterranean – and each year the birds have to overcome this twice. Because flying over large stretches of open water is a hazard – for small birds there is nowhere to land and rest and even for larger species the lack of land-generated thermals is a problem – they try to minimise the distance covered over sea. The southern coast of Spain, and in particular the area around Gibraltar, act as a funnel for the migrants which concentrate along the Costa del Sol before and after making a crossing. A large proportion of the migrant birds which breed in western Europe use this route. Headlands along the Costa del Sol may also be used as landfalls or embarkation points for migrants. Try visiting Cabo Sacrotil or Cabo de Gata or even the coast at Calahonda (east of Marbella) or Punta Marroqui at Tarifa.

The best time of day to observe newly arrived migrant birds is early in the morning. Many will have crossed the sea at night or in the early morning and spend the first few hours of daylight feeding and resting before continuing their journey. As a general rule, most species tend to occur in the habitat to which they are most suited: warblers and flycatchers will feed in bushes and shrubs, wheatears and wagtails will be found on open land and waders and terns will occur along the coast or around freshwater.

Flamboyant insect camouflage

PEACE AND QUIET

Orchids

It may come as something of a surprise to many people to discover that the Costa del Sol is a wonderful place to find wild orchids. These are not the exotic orchids of cultivation but rather smaller and less spectacular species. What they lack in size, however, they make up for with the extraordinary variety in shapes and patterns of their flowers.

A few species are widespread and can be found close to some of the major resorts. For more variety, however, travel into the hills – especially to areas of limestone – and you will find orchids with names that reflect their extraordinary appearances: naked man orchid, bumblebee orchid and tongue orchid are just three examples.

One of the most characteristic orchid groups of the region are those that belong to the bee orchid family. The flowers have evolved to resemble female bees and wasps – each species looks like a different insect. Male insects are attracted to mate but instead unwittingly carry the pollen to the next flower. In addition to the bee orchid, visitors should find bumblebee orchids, yellow bee orchids, woodcock orchids and mirror orchids – the latter species has a shiny patch on the flower.

Serranía de Ronda

The Serranía de Ronda is a wild and rocky region lying inland from the resorts of Marbella and Torremolinos. The town of Ronda which lies at the heart of the Serranía has itself much to offer the visiting naturalist, and especially the birdwatcher, but it is by exploring the surrounding country that you are most likely to discover a superb range of Spanish birds, as well as fascinating plants.

Ronda is carved in two by the spectacular Tajo gorge. Rock buntings can be seen on rock ledges and blue rock thrushes sing their haunting and rather melancholy song from rocky pinnacles and outcrops. Crag martins, rather sombre relatives of sand martins, feed in small groups close to the rock face, hawking insects on the wing, while Alpine swifts – larger than their common relatives and with a white throat and belly – scythe through the skies at greater speed.

Pride of place, however, must go to the gorge's birds of prey. Lesser kestrels are commonly seen and with luck griffon and black vultures may also circle within view. Black vultures have immense, broad wings and resemble nothing so much as a barn door in flight. You might also see buzzards, booted eagles, golden eagles, short-toed eagles and peregrines.

A few areas of woodland – mainly cork oak or maritime pine but also a few patches of the rare Spanish silver fir – can still be found in the vicinity of Ronda. The woodland floor in these remnant forests is often rich in flowers and these in turn attract a wide variety of butterflies. Woodland birdlife is especially noticeable in spring and may include species such as serin, Sardinian warbler, willow warbler, short-toed tree-creeper, hoopoe, nightingale and Scop's owl. Some of these are more easily heard than seen, however.

FOOD AND DRINK

The culinary choice spans the continents. Costa del Sol caterers have a clientele as different as Arabs and Argentinians, but they satisfy them all. Innovative chefs, like Paul Schiff in his La Hacienda restaurant, create light dishes of an individuality which defies national classification. The places to eat range from the simple to the superb, from a *merendero* (beach restaurant) on the shore at Maro to La Meridiana in Marbella. There is little need to worry about being able to find any particular cuisine, cooking style, ambience or price category, especially along the western part of the coast.

The staple ingredients in much of the basic local cooking are olive oil and garlic, liberally used. The best-known regional speciality is *gazpacho*, a cold cucumber and tomato soup. Onions and peppers also feature strongly, and chicken and pork are the most used meats. The wide choice of fish and shellfish comes from both Mediterranean and Atlantic catches. Sweet dishes and pastries often have Moorish origins. A lot of fruit is grown locally, including subtropical varieties.

Tapas, a choice of tasty snacks served in bars, are an Andaluz invention. Sometimes they are offered free when you buy a drink, but more often you have to pay. Tapas can be a good way of trying out several local specialities without straining your budget or digestion.

Eating 'al aire libre'

Many villages have a *bodega* producing *vino terreno* (wine of the land) for local consumption. It can often be strong and heady but it is always cheap. Málaga's sweet and luscious wine has long been a British favourite. Cádiz province produces sherries, and the Montilla-Moriles district of Córdoba province is another producer of sherry-like wines for drinking before or after a meal. Good white table wines now also come from Montilla-Moriles as well as Cádiz and Huelva provinces. Red and white wines from Rioja and Penedés, the internationally best-known wine regions of Spain, as well as those of other regions, are widely available. So is every other conceivable alcoholic drink, usually served in more generous measure and at lower prices than in other European countries.

FOOD AND DRINK

Paella is a popular staple dish

Food and Drink of La Axarquía

This differs in some ways from what is available on the rest of the Costa del Sol. As you might expect, most coastal menus offer a mixture of international dishes for the unadventurous (or delicate) stomach, together with some of the better known Spanish regional specialities. Traditional local recipes are most likely to be found in the smaller restaurants, and by going inland. Almonds, raisins, honey and the local mountain wine all play a part in the menu. *Ajoblanco* is one of the most popular and typical of Axarquian dishes. Basically it is the same as gazpacho, but with ground almonds instead of tomatoes. It is usually served cold with either peeled grapes or raisins. Another version is the *cachorreña*, or hot gazpacho, which has bread and orange juice added before serving. *Potaje de hinojos* is a thick soup made with fresh fennel. Main courses include *berza*, a

form of stew made with meat, potatoes, green beans, chickpeas, pumpkin and aubergine. *Chivo con salsa de almendras* is goat in a rich sauce made from almonds, garlic, vinegar, bread and olive oil. The humblest dish of the region must be *migas* – usually breadcrumbs, fried in olive oil with garlic and then garnished with olives, small fish or anything that the cook has to hand. Migas make tasty tapas. Popular fish dishes of the area are often quite simple, such as the fried anchovies (*boquerones victorianos*) of Rincón de la Victoria, or *espetos de sardinas*, which are whole sardines cooked over an open fire and found everywhere. Even *fritura malagueña* (mixed fried fish) comes without garnish or sauce here.

Desserts are numerous and include all forms of pastry, cake, bun and biscuit, usually very sweet. Often these are specially made for local fiestas. One strange surprise you may come across is the *batatillas de miel* (sweet potatoes in molasses) of Frigiliana.

Almost every village has its own bodega. The local wines, mostly made from the moscatel grape, are justifiably popular. These range from dry table wines to very sweet dessert wines, the most outstanding of which are produced in Frigiliana and Competa.

SHOPPING

Spain's reputation for cheap shopping is generally a thing of the past, but so is its notoriety for poor quality. It is a sound policy to look for good or novel items of Andaluz or Spanish design and manufacture, as well as traditional craft products, and other work by creative people living locally. Clothes can be an excellent buy: Spain's fashion designers are now among the bright stars on the international scene. See also **Shopping** sections under entries for individual towns.

ACCOMMODATION

Officially registered accommodation in Málaga province provides some 84,000 places, 53,000 in hotels, 19,000 in apartments, and 12,000 in camping sites. If you include apartments and villas specifically built for short rentals, the total comes to around 400,000 places. Added to those are private properties which owners make available for rental when they are not in residence.

A lot of visitors never have to choose: they go to their own place, or book a package which includes travel and accommodation. If you want to make your own selection, you may see advertisements for private lettings in quality newspapers in your country. Alternatively, make enquiries on arrival at property agents in towns and urbanisations. Remember that holiday operators get very much better deals for hotel, apartment and villa accommodation than you are likely to get yourself. Off-season, you may be able to negotiate a reduced price, especially for longer stays.

Do not be carried away by holiday euphoria into signing contracts for private rentals without clarifying some essential points. What does the rental include? Are charges for electricity, water, gas, cleaning and so on separate, and if so, what are they? Check the meter readings, if any, on your arrival and departure. What is the inventory and what are the

Hostals offer budget accommodation

charges for damages? Always check that the place has adequate security, and be sure to lock it when you leave. Officially registered accommodation is available in: *Hoteles* and *Hotel Apartamentos*, 1- to 5-star (5-star *Gran Lujo* is the top); *Apartamentos Turisticos*, 1- to 3-key; *Hostales*, 1- to 3-star; *Pensiones, Fondas* (Inns) and *Casas de Huéspedes* (Guest Houses); Camping, 1- to 3-class. Prices are officially registered annually. They should be on display, and should be state the rate of value-added tax (IVA). Spain's tourist office in your country and local tourist offices will provide information about officially registered accommodation, but they will not make bookings. There are *Paradores Nacionales*, state-run hotels of

high standard, at Málaga, Antequera, Torremolinos and Nerja. See also **Accommodation** under entries for individual towns.

NIGHTLIFE

All along the coast there are nightspots of every sort, where you can be entertained by others or make your own action and fun. There are bars specifically catering to different nationalities, with national drinks and singalongs; and there are piano bars, jazz bars, bars with small cabaret shows, and glitzy music bars. Discos vary from the run-of-the-mill to the most modern multi-space venues with the latest light, laser and sound equipment. Flamenco *tablaos* are very popular but some have diluted their authenticity in order to meet foreigners' tastes. Fortuna Night Club at Torrequebrada, Benalmádena, presents a big international floorshow.

Málaga is best for anything cultural, and Marbella is next best. For nightlife Málaga offers a big choice of places, mostly frequented by local people. Marbella's top spots are exclusive, pricey and cliquey. International music stars doing European tours increasingly include either Marbella or Málaga in their itinerary. Torremolinos offers the most variety: from mediocre to brash, cosmopolitan, exhilarating, exotic or erotic. It is also the town which caters most for gay people.

Nightspots cater to a range of tastes

WEATHER AND WHEN TO GO

Simply stated, the weather is unbeatable in Europe – the climate has been the main reason for the Costa del Sol's development as a top tourist zone. Average temperatures reach a peak of 85°F (30°C) in August and a low of 66°F (18°C) in January. In winter, which sees nearly all the rainfall, the backdrop of mountains protects the coast from cold interior winds. In summer, sea breezes have a cooling effect. The interior beyond the mountain backdrop gets very hot in summer, reaching temperatures as high as 110°F (45°C) in some places.

All this means that the Costa del Sol is a destination for any time, depending on your interests and when you are free to go. Some restaurants, shops, hotels, sports and leisure amenities close from October to Easter. During August, people flock to the coast from inland towns and cities, and many businesses are closed.

After the catch, mending the nets

HOW TO BE A LOCAL

The question is, which type of local? There are many expatriate communities, and they are usually happy to accept newcomers, especially of their own nationality. Being a local can mean behaving much as you would at home. The real locals – the Andalucians – can seem a world apart.

Tourists are the latest in a series of invasions which Andalucians have been inclined not to resist. They have let the climate, the beauty of the land and their own inscrutability and charm do the work of moulding the invader to a gentler, more courteous behaviour, and a world view closer to their own.

It is meaningless to generalise about all six and a half million Andalucians, though Nikos Kazantzakis did so when he wrote, 'The Andalucians, with

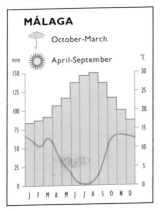

MÁLAGA

☂ October-March

☀ April-September

mm		°C
150		30
125		25
100		20
75		15
50		10
25		5
0		0

J F M A M J J A S O N D

HOW TO BE A LOCAL

Away from the coast: another world

their warm, pleasant climate and their pathos-steeped souls – sensual like the Arabs, uneducated yet cultivated, lazy, yet at the same time, in their passionate moments, fierce, anarchic, fiery'. All that could be equally true of other peoples. What is undeniable is that the indigenous people of southern Spain have absorbed character traits and customs from others, including conquerors and settlers from Castile and northern parts of Spain, and most of all from almost 800 years of Moorish rule. Along the coastal region especially, it is Moorish culture which has left the deepest mark on individual and communal behaviour. Precisely what Andalucians will think about their region and people will depend on where they come from, what province, what *pueblo* (village) or *barrio* (part of a city).

A perspective of life and the world is formed within the family, still very much a matriarchal unit in which the mother is both the most revered and the most hardworked. Next in influence is the perception of the community, which can be very different in isolated pueblos, city barrios, or tourist resorts. Then there is the close and closed circle of friends in which an Andaluz also finds solidarity and comfort. These three mingled influences protect a person, but their strength can also strangle fresh thought and progress. Foreigners in search of acceptance by an Andaluz must somehow gain acceptance within one sphere of influence and then wriggle their way into the others, perhaps by *enchufes* – introductions – the Andaluz means for social and career progress. This may seem baffling, and many outsiders do not even try. Even many of those who have settled on the Costa del Sol tend to mix only with people of their own nationality. Many make little effort to understand local ways or even the language, and are scornful of Andalucians and their 'laziness'. If you want to get to know local people, you will need a different, more flexible attitude. Be prepared to be perplexed. Forget all preconceptions about Andalucians, especially the one that they are lazy. Be dismissive of time constraints, and keep your temper when everything closes during the siesta or on a local fiesta day you did not know about.

Do not object to noise but add to it and be demonstrative of emotion. Join in enthusiastically by living life to the full and for the moment, not caring about tomorrow. Flashing wealth around will not gain you acceptance, but if you have talent, you may become known as un listo, 'a clever one', by waxing into verse, bursting into song, or making music (and outsmarting the authorities). Laugh at jokes about death and make your own humour black and fatalistic.

Remember that the collective sanction or praise of the community is usually worth more than the sanction of authorities or any outside recognition. Join intercommunity rivalry by being as rude as local people about the next barrio, pueblo, town or province; but praise the place where you are and its province, and always praise Andalucía as a whole. Avoid discussion about local politics and personalities, no matter how disparaging the company you are in may be about them.

Admire a man's virility and a woman's fertility; the dress and deportment of both; a woman's housekeeping and cooking skills (activities in which macho men do not engage themselves). Praise an Andaluz's mother, children and prize animals; but men should not overdo the praise of an Andaluz man's wife. If you praise her husband too much, a wife will view you sceptically, for she is wise to his foibles.

To be a real local, you will probably have to forget the norms of your home society. Remember, Andalucía is a foreign and ancient land, closer to Africa than Europe.

CHILDREN

Children are made to feel very welcome on the Costa del Sol. Like most Mediterranean people, Andalucians tend to idolise the very young, and usually pay them more attention than their parents. Local children stay up late, often having a siesta to compensate, and it is not unusual to see them dropping off to sleep in a restaurant well after midnight, while the conversation and merrymaking of the adults goes on unabated.

That said, parents should make the fullest enquiries in advance about exactly what they want for their children, rather than blaming the resort or accommodation if the children do not have a good time. Some places cater especially well for the young, with amusements, events, special meal times and menus, babysitting and listening services. Most of the towns have playparks. They also have *guarderías* (daytime care centres) and babysitting services. Information and advice about these are best sought from local tourist offices, which can also advise on any entertainments arranged by municipalities or other organisations. Fiestas and ferias often contain a strong element of diversions for children. High standard sports amenities are provided in many places, for children practising a favourite sport or learning a new one. Aquaparks operate during the main season at Torre del Mar, Torremolinos and Fuengirola-Mijas. Torremolinos also has the Treasure Island amusement park for children; Tivoli World is a large amusement park at Benalmádena. Fuerte El Dorada, a mock Wild West fort which stages performances, is easy to reach from Torre del Mar. There are organised 'burro safaris' (donkey excursions) on a farm near Coín, about which holiday operators and travel agents will provide information. A beach or a swimming pool, followed by familiar food and drinks, may be all that many children want, and the Costa del Sol is good at providing those things. If new food and cultural experiences are required, however, those are in easy reach as well. There are plenty of memorable places to visit inland (see **Excursions**). Remember that this is the 'Coast of the Sun'. Over exposure can be painful or dangerous. Use sunhats and a high factor sun cream or lotion, and let children get a tan gradually.

TIGHT BUDGET

As a start you should investigate what budget holiday packages exist to the Costa del Sol, and find out about low-cost charter flights to Málaga from your country.

• Avoid taking taxis whenever possible. Local bus services are especially cheap, as is the half-hourly train service that connects all points between Málaga and Fuengirola (including the airport).

• If you consider renting a car for a day or two, avoid the big international companies and compare prices carefully among the local firms.

• Beware hidden car-rental costs (daily insurance, distance, etc), and be sure to enquire about special weekend rates.

• Often renting a bicycle or moped can work out more economical – and fun – for short excursions.

• Renting a minibus can be good value if you are part of a group.

• Look for accommodation in the old parts of town.

• Avoid the star-rated hotels and look for those buildings showing the blue signs – CH (casa huéspedes) or F (fonda). These will be cheap, simple and usually family-run.

• If you are travelling with someone else, and you wish to stay for more than a couple of days, it may be economical to rent an apartment. Enquire in bars and pubs rather than at an estate agent.

• Look for restaurants offering a menu of the day. These can be up to 30 per cent cheaper than the normal *à la carte* prices.

• Some bars offer such large tapas with a beer or wine that a couple of rounds make a substitute for a meal.

• Meat, fish and vegetables are best bought in the daily market, as are the ingredients for a moneysaving picnic.

• A visit to the weekly flea-market will help save pesetas on most basic necessities as well as certain souvenirs and handicrafts.

• Few tourist attractions are free along the coast, but entrance fees to museums and monuments are usually very reasonable. Enquire at the local tourist office for exact details and a free map of the area.

• Sports facilities can be very expensive, but most towns have a municipal sports centre which is open to visitors. These can be very modern and comprehensive, and are likely to offer the best value for money.

• For local flavour as well as lower prices, steer clear of the beachfront and search out one of the small hole-in-the-wall back street bars. (Just follow the sounds of the blaring TV and clacking dominoes!)

• Local *vino terreno* (country wine) or *una caña* (draught beer) will be the cheapest on the pricelist.

• Keep an eye open for other bars offering 'Happy Hour' discounts – usually two drinks for the price of one.

• Some discothèques charge hefty entrance fees (with one free drink), but sometimes girls will be allowed in free. Look for the touts who hand out free tickets during the summer.

SPECIAL EVENTS

It sometimes seems that any day, somewhere in Andalucía, there is a celebration. On 6 January, **Cabalgata de los Reyes**, the Three Kings parade on floats throwing sweets to bystanders. **Carnival** closes on Ash Wednesday (February/ March) after days of colourful and hectic merrymaking. In their celebration of **Semana Santa** (Holy Week) Andalucians almost surpass themselves in a

Parading spectacular devotion

display of religious devotion verging on the pagan in its ritual and zeal. In even the humblest village an image of the Virgin or Christ will be taken from the church and borne aloft in rudimentary procession. Larger communities will have more than one image carried on richly decorated *pasos* (floats) by different *cofradías* (brotherhoods), with berobed and hooded *nazarenos* (penitents), following behind. Muffled drums beat sonorously and bystanders call out haunting *saetas* in devotion. The smell of incense and candlewax hangs in the air. Seville mounts the biggest procession, but those in Málaga and Granada are equally spectacular.

Some places celebrate **Cruces de Mayo** at the beginning of May, when crosses are decorated with real or artificial flowers. For **Corpus Christi** in May or June, the streets are strewn with flowers. On the night of 23 June effigies of Júas (Judas) are burned to open **San Juan's** celebration the next day. The patron of sailors and fishermen, **Virgen el Carmen**, has her day on 16 July, when there are maritime processions and beachside celebrations in all the coastal towns. Many places have **romerías** at different times, with colourful, lively processions to a local shrine followed by music, dance, food and wine. All places will have one or more **fiestas** in honour of patron saints. Many also have an annual week-long **feria**, which includes fairgrounds, processions in local costume, flamenco, verdiales,

cultural events, gastronomic events, bullfights, fireworks and more.

Verdiales are a folk custom unique to Málaga province, performed by brightly and oddly dressed groups called *pandas*. Music from an assortment of instruments, with violins keeping the rhythm, accompanies singers and dancers. Verdiales are part of many celebrations, and on 28 December pandas meet for a competition in the Montes de Málaga. For local celebrations, see **Special Events** under entries for individual towns.

SPORT

Watersports and many others, such as bowling, horseriding, tennis and squash, are widely available. See **Sport** sections under entries for the main resorts. One sport stands out: not for nothing is this called the Costa del Golf. Serious enthusiasts will get to know about courses along the whole coast by reading their regular golfing magazines and club newsletters, talking to other players, asking for information at tourist offices or buying *Costa Golf* or other golfing magazines published locally. The Patronato Provincial de Turismo publishes a golf leaflet which gives details of the clubs. Courses sometimes get so heavily booked by members that visiting players can only get a game in the early morning or during the hottest part of a summer day. To avoid this, you may want to book games in advance of your arrival.

DIRECTORY

Contents

Gaucín, one of the 'pueblos blancos'

Arriving

Entry Formalities

You require a valid passport to enter Spain. Nationals of European Community countries, and of some other countries, do not need a visa for stays of up to 90 days. It is always wise to check the current situation with the Spanish tourist office or Spanish consulate in your country. Visitors from most countries do not require any medical documents but, if in any doubt, check at one of the above places.

By air

Iberia, Spain's national airline, and the airlines of other countries, operate direct connections between Málaga and most European capital cities. Charter companies operate connections with a number of European airports, especially in the summer. Intercontinental connections will be increasing on completion of a new terminal building. Connections with Spanish cities are by Iberia or Aviaco, its

DIRECTORY

affiliate. The airport is five miles (8km) southwest of the city off the N340 highway, and has the usual amenities of a Grade 1 international airport. Porters charge by the number of bags. A train service connects with the city and with Torremolinos and Fuengirola. There is also a scheduled bus connection with the city.

By bus
There are regular bus services from a number of countries. Enquire in your country.

By car
On completion of the new highway network, projected for the end of 1991, a driver should be able to go from Copenhagen, Frankfurt, Paris or Rome to Málaga and the western Costa del Sol without having to stop for a single traffic light.

By rail
Renfe is Spain's national rail company. There is a choice of routes from Spain's northern border to Málaga: the Talgo trains are the fastest and most comfortable. A new high-speed train will cut the journey from Madrid to Seville from around seven hours to two hours and forty-five minutes.

By sea
Transmediterránea run a connection between the Canary Islands and Barcelona via Málaga and Cádiz.

Camping
There are some 12,000 places at sites in Málaga province, along the coast and inland.
Information will be available from the Spanish Tourist Office in your country.

Chemist See Pharmacies

Consulates
These are all in Málaga unless otherwise indicated.
Canada, Plaza de la Malagueta 3 (tel: 22 33 46).
Republic of Ireland, c/ General Mola, Santa Mónica, Fuengirola (tel: 72 25 04).
United Kingdom, Edificio Duquesa, c/ Duquesa Parcent (tel: 21 75 71).
US, Centro Commercial Las Rampas, Fase II, 1267, Fuengirola (tel: 48 58 91).

Explore inland on a local bus

Crime

Snatching of handbags and cameras, picking of pockets, running off with unattended luggage or bags and breaking into cars are the principal crimes against visitors. Muggings to steal jewellery and cash do also happen, more so in lonely streets, parks and seedier parts of cities. Málaga and Seville have had the biggest problems with this type of crime, which is usually committed by young people to finance a drug dependence. Seville has also spawned the *semaforos*, who smash windows of cars stopped at traffic lights, grab what they can and dash off on a moped or motorcycle. Although the precautions which visitors can take are obvious, here are a few reminders. Deposit valuables (travellers' cheques, cash, passports and so on) in a safety deposit box wherever you are staying. Wear handbags and cameras across your chest and wallets in front trouser pockets. Do not be ostentatious with jewellery or cash. Keep an eye on your parcels and luggage, and do not leave valuables in a car (even a bag holding nothing of value, but left in sight, may be a temptation for a break-in). Avoid lonely, seedy and dark areas, and make use of taxis late at night.

Customs Regulations

Ask for information on the current allowances and regulations from the airline or holiday operator, or from the Spanish tourist office or Spanish consulate in your country.

Disabled People

Newer buildings are likely to have amenities such as ramps, wider doorways, and toilets. Wheelchair rental: Sr Valerzuela, Clinica Santa Elena, Los Alemos, Torremolinos (tel: 38 62 66). For general advice send a large stamped addressed envelope to RADAR, 25 Mortimer Street, London W1N 8AB (tel: (071) 637 5400).

Driving

Breakdown

Breakdown vehicles are called *gruas*. The **Real Automovil Club de España**, Plaza Uncibay 3, Málaga (tel: 21 42 60), has reciprocal arrangements with motoring organisations elsewhere, and can advise in case of need.

Car rental

International firms operate on the Costa del Sol, and you can make bookings with them in your home country. Holiday operators have car rental schemes, and airlines offer 'fly-drive' deals. Hiring from a smaller local firm is usually much cheaper.

In the travel pages of newspapers and at the Spanish tourist office in your home country, you should find information about firms which make block bookings for cars with rental operators on the Costa del Sol, and pass on part of their very favourable rates. On the Costa del Sol, you can pick up details at tourist offices and travel agents.

Documents

Licences issued by European Community countries are

acceptable. People from other countries should have an international driving licence, usually obtainable from a motoring organisation in their country.

Fuel
The types are normal (92 octane); super (96 octane); gas-oil (diesel); and *sin plomo* (lead-free – happily increasingly available).

Parking
Spaces are indicated by blue road and kerb markings, and tickets are bought from machines on the pavement.

Road signs and rules
Generally these are in line with those of other European countries, with eccentricities which are only comprehensible after exposure to them. Obtain a Bail Bond before you leave home; otherwise you could be arrested if involved in an accident. Spain's Ministry of Transport publishes a small leaflet of advice for drivers. Try to get one at frontier posts or tourist offices. If you are driving to Spain, take advice and get information from a motoring organisation in your country and buy appropriate insurance.

Electricity
220/230 volts AC and 110/120 in some bathrooms and older buildings. Plugs have two round pins.

Emergency Telephone Numbers
Policia Nacional 091
Policia Local 092
These 24-hour numbers will not necessarily connect you with the nearest station but will get your message relayed.

Entertainment Information
Daily newspapers, monthly magazines (see **Media**), and the free monthly *Costa del Sol – What's On*, published by the Patronato Provincial de Turismo, provide listings. Look at billboards and pick up leaflets and information from tourist offices.

Entry Formalities See Arriving

Health
Residents of European Community countries are entitled to medical treatment from the Spanish health service if they show form E110, E111 or E112 (obtain this before leaving home). But the best advice for all foreign visitors to Spain is to buy a travel insurance policy from a reputable company which provides comprehensive cover in case of accident and illness. Ask the insurance company exactly what procedure should be followed in case of need. It is also wise to carry a photocopy of prescriptions for any medication which you are taking.
Health problems are most likely to arise from too much sun, or from over-indulgence in drink and food by people in a holiday mood. In summer, they may be from too much sun and eating mayonnaise or 'sad' salads and tapas. Unfamiliar tap water can cause a bad reaction, so stick to bottled water.

Hospitals
There are a number of private hospitals and dental clinics to which you may be

Fishy business for the locals in the streets of Nerja

recommended locally, and public hospitals with departments for *urgencias* (emergencies) in Málaga, Vélez-Málaga, Antequera, Ronda and Marbella (under construction).

Holidays
Besides the variable dates of **Easter** and **Whitsun**, the principal holidays are:
Año Nuevo (1 January)
Día de los Reyes (6 Janaury)
Día de Andalucía (28 February)
San José (19 March)
Día del Trabajo (1 May)
San Juan (24 June)
Santiago (25 July)
Asunción (15 August)
Hispanidad (12 October)
Todos los Santos (1 November)
Immaculada Concepción (8 December)
Navidad (25 December).
Every town and village has its own feast days, when you may find everything closed.

Lost Property
Oficinas de Objetos Perdidos (Lost Property Offices) are located at *Ayuntamientos* (Town Halls). Advise your consulate about any loss of personal documents and, if necessary contact credit card companies.

Media

Periodicos (newspapers)
Many newspapers from other European countries are available by the afternoon. International editions are on sale in the morning. The liberal *El País* is the national daily with the widest respect internationally, and publishes a Seville edition. So do other national dailies, like the conservative *ABC* and the middle-ground *Diario 16*. *El Sol de Andalucía* is very good for coverage of the region. *Sur*, published in Málaga, has a free weekly edition in English.

Revistas (magazines)
Spain publishes a plethora of magazines. The weekly *Cambio 16* is a respected news magazine in the *Times/ Newsweek* format. For sensationalism and scandal *Hola*

is the leader. Among a number of foreign language magazines published on the Costa del Sol are *Lookout* (English), *Aktuelle* (German) and *Solkysten* (Scandinavian).

Television
Two channels are national and state-run; one is controlled by the Junta de Andalucía. There are also private networks, stations run by municipal authorities and a host of satellite programmes.

Radio
Foreign, national, regional, local – public and private – stations vie for space. English language stations include BBC World Service on shortwave 17705khz (day) and 15070khz (night).

Money Matters

Banks
There seems to be one on every street corner, and foreign

Traditional designs and local views on hand-painted ceramics

names like Barclays and NatWest are increasingly evident. Savings banks, mostly also offering exchange facilities, are called *cajas*. *Open:* Monday to Friday 08.30–14.00hrs, Saturday (except June to September) 08.30–13.00hrs. Money exchange facilities are available outside these hours at Málaga airport and El Corte Inglés. Cashpoints issuing money with use of a credit card and PIN are plentiful.

Credit Cards
The major credit, charge and direct debit cards are widely accepted, but not at fuel stations. Make a note of your credit card numbers and emergency telephone numbers to contact in case of loss, and keep it with your passport.

Currency
The peseta is available in the following denominations: notes 10,000, 5,000, 2,000, 1,000; coins 500, 200, 100, 50, 25, 10, 5 and 1.

Tax
Value-added tax, called IVA, is currently applied at six per cent on most goods and services and at 12 or 33 per cent on luxury items and some services. People resident outside Spain can gain exemption from tax on large individual purchases. Shops will provide information. But think about what tax the goods may incur on importation into your home country.

Opening Times
See also **Money Matters** and **Post Office**.
Generally shops are open Monday to Saturday from between 09.00 and 10.00 to 13.30 or 14.00hrs and again from 17.00 to between 20.00 and 21.00hrs. Hypermarkets and department stores are open from 10.00 to 21.00 or 22.00hrs. Business offices work Monday to Friday and general hours are 09.00–14.00 and 16.00–20.00hrs. In the summer many businesses work *horas intensivas*, 08.00–15.00hrs. Official organisations are generally open to the public from Monday to Friday 09.00–14.00hrs.

Personal Safety
See **Crime** above, and take the same care of yourself and others as you would at home. The greatest natural danger is the sun: use a high factor sun cream to start with, and allow yourself to become used to it gradually.

Pharmacies
As well as selling prescription medicines, they will provide free advice about minor injuries and ailments and suggest a non-prescription treatment from their stocks. They are easily identified by a big green or red cross sign and follow normal shopping hours. At other times they will display a sign indicating the nearest *farmacia de guardia*, which will be open. Local papers also list these.

Places of Worship
The great majority of churches are Catholic. In some churches Catholic masses are said in other languages at specified times. Other denominations and faiths with communities on the Costa del Sol are: Anglican, Church of Jesus Christ of Latter-Day Saints, Christian Science, Church of Scotland, Evangelical, German Protestant, Jehovah's Witness, Jewish, Muslim, Scottish Presbyterian and Swedish Lutheran. Tourist offices and consulates will provide information on places and times of worship.

Police
Officers of the three police organisations have different, sometimes confusingly overlapping roles. See also **Emergency Telephone Numbers.**
Policia Local These are the municipal police, and are mainly responsible for traffic. They have blue uniforms and white checked bands on their vehicles and caps.
Policia Nacional Spain's national police, also in blue, are responsible for law and order

DIRECTORY

and internal security. It is to them that you should report a crime or loss and make a *denuncia* (statement).

Guardia Civil Officers in green uniforms are mostly seen at border posts, in country areas and along the coastline. One branch is responsible for highway patrols.

Post Office

The *Correos* is usually clearly signposted in the towns. *Open:* Monday to Friday 09.00–14.00 hrs, Saturday 09.00–13.00 hrs. If you want mail to be sent, it should be addressed to you at Lista de Correos, followed by the postcode and town name, Provincia de Málaga, España. Take personal identification when collecting. Post boxes are yellow and some have different sections for different destinations. *Sellos* (stamps) can also be bought at *estancos* (tobacconists).

Public Transport

Air

Travel agents are the best free source of information. Foreign airlines have offices at Málaga airport. The main office of Iberia is at Calle Molina Lario 13, Málaga. For information and reservations, tel: 21 37 31.

Bus

There is a comprehensive and reliable bus network operated by different companies along the coast and to inland towns and villages. Fares are very reasonable. Go to the local bus station to get details of routes.

Taxis

Only use taxis which display a licence issued by the local authority. Taxis show a green light when available for hire and can be flagged down in the street. In cities and large towns standard rates are shown on the meter and there are supplements for baggage or for trips departing from railway stations and the airport. When taxis are not metered, you should determine the price of the journey in advance.

Trains

Full information can be obtained from travel agents and from Renfe stations in Málaga, Torremolinos and Fuengirola.

Senior Citizens

Ask travel agents about special package holidays on the Costa del Sol for senior citizens. The climate and facilities make it a popular destination, and special low-cost, long-stay holidays are available for senior citizens in the winter months – still warm, but not oppressively so.

Student and Youth Travel

Special facilities and programmes are limited. Ask specialist travel agencies, tour operators and youth organisations in your own country. The main advantage for young people is that low-cost package deals are available. See also **Tight Budget.**

Telephones

Access codes: from Australia dial 0011; Canada 011; New Zealand 00; UK 010; US 011. To ring from Spain, dial: Australia 61; Canada 1; New Zealand 64; UK 44; US 1.

The code for Málaga (city and province) is 952 and is used for calls from other provinces. To call a Málaga number from outside Spain dial the international service code applicable in your country, then 34 (Spain), 52 (Málaga) and the six digit number. Public phone booths are plentiful. They take 100, 25 and 5 peseta coins and some accept credit cards. Instructions for use are displayed in a number of languages, as are provincial and international dialling codes. Many bars also have telephones for use by customers. To make direct international calls put at least 200 pesetas in the groove at the top (or in the slot of some telephones), dial 07 and await for a changed tone, then dial the country code, town code (without initial 0) and number. At the Telefónica *locutorios* you can get assistance and make reversed charge calls. Otherwise you pay after your call. A cheap rate applies from

22.00 to 08.00 hrs. For telephone information, dial 003.

Telefax, Telex and Telegrams
Business bureaux offer telefax and (some) telex services. Telegram offices are usually at post offices. For telegrams by telephone tel: 22 20 00.

Time
Like most of Europe, Spain is two hours ahead of GMT (Greenwich Mean Time) in the summer and one hour ahead in the winter.

Tipping
Although most hotel and restaurant bills will include a service charge, you may still want to give a tip of between five and 10 per cent in restaurants and for special services in hotels. At bars leave less than five per cent from whatever change you get. The same applies to taxis. Other people who usually get tips are carpark attendants, doormen, hairdressers, lavatory

Children enjoy the donkey work

DIRECTORY

attendants, shoeshines and tour guides.

Toilets
Public lavatories are few and far between. There are toilet facilities at department stores, some museums and places of interest. Bars and restaurants have facilities for customers.

Tourist Offices
Contact Turespaña at:
Australia 203 Castlereagh Street, Suite 21, Sydney NSW 2000 (tel: (02) 264 7966).
Canada 102 Bloor Street West, 14th Floor, Toronto (tel: (416) 961 3131).
UK 57–8 St James Street, London SW1A 1LD (tel: (071) 499 0901).
US 665 Fifth Avenue, New York 10022 (tel: (212) 759 8822); 8383 Wilshire Bvd, Suite 960, Beverley Hills, California 90211 (tel: (213) 658 7188).

Málaga has tourist offices at the airport (tel: 24 00 00 extension 6433), bus station (tel: 35 00 61) and at Calle Nicasio 7 (tel: 21 34 45). Written enquiries can be made to the Patronato Provincial de Turismo, Calle Compositor Lehmberg Ruiz 3, 29007, Málaga.

Elsewhere
Antequera Palacio de Nájera, Calle Coso Viejo s/n (tel: 84 21 80).
Benalmádena Costa Carretera Nacional 340; Museo Arqueológico Benalmádena Pueblo.
Córdoba Calle Torijos 10 (tel: 47 12 35); Ayuntamiento, Plaza de Judá (tel: 47 20 00).
Estepona Paseo Marítimo, Pedro Manrique (tel: 80 09 13).
Fuengirola and Mijas Parque de España, Avenida Condes de San Isidro (tel: 47 61 66).
Granada Casa de los Tiros, 19 Calle Pavaneras (tel: 22 10 22).
Marbella Avenida Miguel Cano 1, Marbella (tel: 77 14 42).
Nerja Calle Puerta del Mar 4 (tel: 52 15 31).
Ronda Plaza de España 1 (tel: 87 12 72).
Seville Avenida de la Constitución 21 (tel: 422 1404); Paseo de las Delicias s/n (tel: 423 4465).
Torre del Mar Avenida de Andalucia (tel: 54 11 04).
Torremolinos Calle Guetaria s/n, La Nogalera (tel: 38 15 78); Calle Casablanca 27 (tel: 37 11 59).

It's a frame-up: personalised posters

LANGUAGE

Andalucians speak Castilian, the 'standard' Spanish. Words are often similar to those of other European languages, especially French and Italian. The hardest part is learning the pronunciation. The main rules are given here. One thing to beware of: many Andalucians pronounce 'c' and 'z' like a hard 's' sound, instead of the usual lisping 'th' (see below). They may also clip the ends of their words and talk rapidly.

Pronunciation

a – as in t<u>a</u>r
e – as in l<u>e</u>t
i – as in mar<u>i</u>ne
o – as in T<u>o</u>m
u – as in r<u>u</u>le
b and **v** – similar, like a soft 'b'
c – like 'th' in <u>th</u>in before 'e' or 'i'; otherwise as in <u>c</u>at
g – like 'ch' in lo<u>ch</u> before 'e' or 'i'; otherwise as in <u>g</u>et
j – like 'ch' in lo<u>ch</u>
ll – like 'lli' in mi<u>lli</u>on
ñ – like 'ni' in o<u>ni</u>on
r – strong and rolled, **rr** more so
z – like 'th' in <u>th</u>in

Stress

Stress the second-to-last syllable if the word ends in n, s, or a vowel. This means nearly all words. Other words have the stress on the last syllable, like Mad<u>ri</u>d, or wherever there is an accent, as in M<u>á</u>laga and C<u>ó</u>rdoba.

Useful words and phrases

hello hola
I am sorry, but I don't speak Spanish lo siento, pero no hablo español
do you speak English? habla inglés?
is there someone who speaks . . .? hay alguien que hable . . .
yes/no sí/no
excuse me, I don't understand perdón, no comprendo
please speak slowly por favor, hable despacio
thank you (very much) (muchas) gracias
you're welcome/think nothing of it de nada
good morning buenos días
good afternoon buenas tardes
good evening buenas noches
I am/my name is soy . . . /me llamo . . .
what is your name? como se llama usted?
how are you? como está?
I am . . . estoy . . .

LANGUAGE

very well muy bien
I (don't) know (something) (no) sé
I (don't) know (a person) (no) conozco
all right vale/de acuerdo
good luck buena suerte
goodbye adiós
see you again hasta luego
where is . . .? donde está?
is it far/near? está lejos/cerca?
very muy
left/right/ahead/at the end izquierda/derecha/delante/al final

avenue/boulevard/road/street/ passage/square avenida/paseo/ carretera/calle/pasaje/plaza
countryside/mountain (mountains)/ hill/river/stream campo/montaña (sierra)/colina/río/arroyo
castle/church/monastery/palace/ school castillo/iglesia/ monasterio/palacio/escuela

open abierto
closed cerrado
hour/day/week/month/year hora/ día/semana/mes/año
Monday to Sunday lunes, martes, miercoles, jueves, viernes, sábado, domingo
yesterday/today/tomorrow ayer/ hoy/mañana
last night/tonight anoche/esta noche

the weekend el fin de semana
last week/next week semana pasada/semana próxima
early/late temprano/tarde

I would like . . . me gustaría . . .
do you have . . .? tiene . . .?
there is (not) (no) hay
how much is? cuánto es/vale/ cuesta?
expensive/cheap caro/barato
short/long corto/largo
enough/too much bastante/ demasiado
more/less más/menos
good/better bueno/mejor
big/bigger grande/más grande
small/smaller pequeño/más pequeño
nothing more, thank you nada más, gracias

Numbers

1 to 10 uno, dos, tres, cuatro, cinco, seis, siete, ocho, nueve, diez
11 to 19 once, doce, trece, catorce, quince, dieciseis, diecisiete, dieciocho, diecinueve
20 to 100 veinte, treinta, cuarenta, cincuenta, sesenta, setenta, ochenta, noventa, cien, doscientos
500 quinientos
1,000 mil

INDEX/ACKNOWLEDGEMENTS

The Automobile Association wishes to thank the following photographers and libraries for their assistance in the preparation of this book:

JENS POULSEN took all the photographs not listed below (© AA PHOTO LIBRARY).

AA PHOTO LIBRARY 96 Seville, Plaza de España, 97 Seville.

INTERNATIONAL PHOTOBANK Cover Nerja, 4 Ronda, 6 Benalmádena, 7 Málaga, 8 Nerja, 14 Fuengirola, 15 Donkey taxi, 17

Casares, 30 Málaga city hall, 33 Málaga city centre, 41 San Isidro Festival, 52 Torremolinos, Carihuela beach, 54 Torremolinos, 59 Benalmádena Marina, 60 Fuengirola harbour, 94 Ronda, Tajo Gorge, 106 Paella, 119 Nerja, 120 Ceramics, 123 Children on donkeys.

NATURE PHOTOGRAPHERS LTD 91 Alhambra at night (C Grey-Wilson), 99 Broom (N A Callow), 100 Bee-eater (P R Sterry), 101 Cork oak (K J Carlson), 102 Birthwort (C Grey-Wilson), 103 Two-tailed pasha (K J Carlson).